C903602224

KU-168-251

METT   AND

LIBRARIES NI
WITHDRAWN FROM STOCK

Entrelac Knitting

40 Stunning Projects With Textured, Diamond-Pattern Designs

Search Press

First published in Great Britain in 2020 by
Search Press Ltd
Wellwood, North Farm Road
Tunbridge Wells, Kent TN2 3DR

Originally published in Norwegian as *Pinnedans*.

Also published in the United States of America in 2020 by
Trafalgar Square Books
North Pomfret, Vermont 05055

Copyright © 2018 Mette Hovden, Heidi Eikeland, and
Cappelen Damm AS
English translation © 2019 Trafalgar Square Books

All rights reserved. No part of this book, text, photographs
or illustrations may be reproduced or transmitted in any form
or by any means by print, photoprint, microfilm, microfiche,
photocopier, internet or in any way known or as yet unknown,
or stored in a retrieval system, without written permission
obtained beforehand from Search Press. Printed in China.

ISBN: 978-1-78221-865-4

The Publishers and author can accept no responsibility for
any consequences arising from the information, advice or
instructions given in this publication.

Readers are permitted to reproduce any of the items/patterns
in this book for their personal use, or for the purposes of selling
for charity, free of charge and without the prior permission of
the Publishers. Any use of the items/patterns for commercial
purposes is not permitted without the prior permission of
the Publishers.

Suppliers
For details of suppliers, please visit the Search Press website:
www.searchpress.com

TABLE OF CONTENTS

PREFACE

Why write a book about entrelac knitting? Because there are few patterns for it, because it is an old technique on the way to being forgotten, and not least because it is unbelievably fun to knit! In order for knowledge about entrelac to survive, the knitting world must have patterns to knit from. You can try the technique at a workshop by knitting a swatch, but it's even more fun when you knit a wearable garment. We previously published the book *Kontstrikk, enklere enn du tror* [Entrelac: Easier than You Think]. That book was intended as a small handy guide with short, simple patterns. The response was bigger than we could have hoped for, increasing our desire to write a new book. Then we were contacted by the publisher asking if we had any plans for a new book. Yes, we just needed to get going on it.

To produce a design in one size only is rather straightforward, but adjusting a garment for several sizes presents a series of challenges. Entrelac blocks are geometric shapes with a set height and width, and that adds to the difficulty. Hence, the work behind even a simple garment takes a lot of time. Without the help of test knitters and sample knitters, we'd never have made it. Without each other, we wouldn't have made it either. A sister you can rely on to help is worth her weight in gold so the hours devoted to the work don't add up to something astronomical.

With this book, we hope that many will discover how fantastic entrelac knitting is, and that way we'll have contributed to saving the technique from oblivion.

Without the support and understanding of our families, we would not have been able to write this book. For how many hours has Mother had that faraway look, sitting deep in concentration over a knitted garment, or getting lost in front of a computer screen? We have no idea—and we don't want to know, either! In any case, one thing the family has learned is to pay attention and wait until Mother has finished knitting a block.

Good luck with your entrelac knitting! We hope you will enjoy this book as much as we have.

Happy knitting from Mette and Heidi

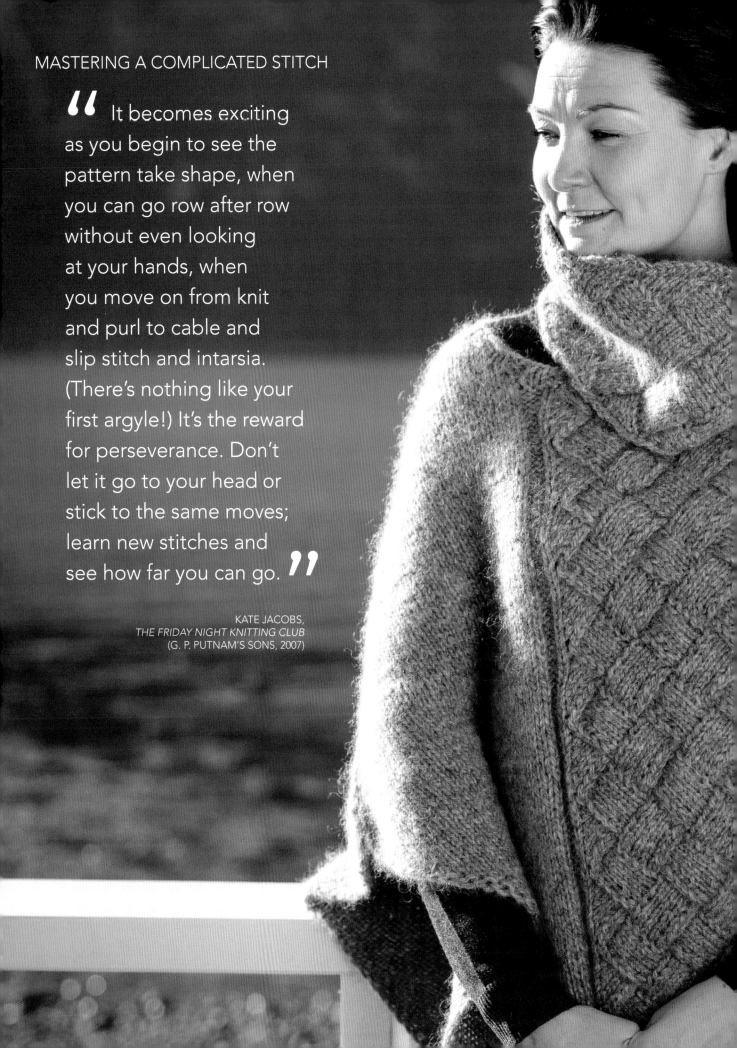

MASTERING A COMPLICATED STITCH

" It becomes exciting as you begin to see the pattern take shape, when you can go row after row without even looking at your hands, when you move on from knit and purl to cable and slip stitch and intarsia. (There's nothing like your first argyle!) It's the reward for perseverance. Don't let it go to your head or stick to the same moves; learn new stitches and see how far you can go. **"**

KATE JACOBS,
THE FRIDAY NIGHT KNITTING CLUB
(G. P. PUTNAM'S SONS, 2007)

Our Story

We are two sisters who share a passion for entrelac knitting. Mette lives in Valldal, and Heidi on the island of Askøy, in Norway. Although there's quite a distance between our homes, the interest in entrelac has grown enormously for both of us and our desire to work together to develop new designs has grown with it over the years.

How did we get started with entrelac?

Entrelac is relatively seldom seen in the modern-day knitting world—so how did we get started with it? It was happenstance, like so much else in life. We have to go a long way back to find the beginning of this history. Mette has knitted since she was little, and by chance she came upon a pattern for a pair of socks knitted in entrelac. They were exactly to her taste, and she had to knit them. She didn't stop with just one pair, but made many pairs of these socks. At first, Mette didn't know the technique was called "entrelac," but she kept with it. She didn't know it was an old traditional design element, or that it was on the official Norwegian "red list" of dying crafts, either. She just started looking for more patterns with these fun blocks, because she liked them—but she didn't find many. At last she found out what she should be looking for: a classic technique called *kontstrikk* in Norwegian and "entrelac" in English. Her search for patterns continued with new energy, but in the end Mette had no choice but to make up her own designs if she wanted to knit more entrelac. Several patterns for small garments followed: socks, mittens, wrist warmers, hats, etc. The garments she knitted caught people's attention; questions about the technique and requests for patterns steadily increased.

Mette worked with entrelac for several years before Heidi showed any interest in it. Heidi was also an enthusiastic knitter, but Mette was alone with entrelac at first. To put it simply, Heidi believed entrelac was too difficult for her to want to try it. Every time Mette made an effort to convince her that it really wasn't so hard, Heidi wouldn't listen. That's how it was for a long time, until Mette had the idea of trying to publish patterns organized by difficulty, preferably in the form of a little book. Heidi quickly offered to support Mette and said she was willing to help—she could copyedit and proofread, at the very least. But Mette thought that Heidi should be a co-author. So, long story short: Heidi had to give in to her big sister's desire and learn how to knit entrelac. That way, Heidi could test-knit patterns for Mette, and eventually produce her own designs. The book *Kontstrikk, enklere enn du tror* [Entrelac: Easier than You Think] was published in January 2015. At the same time, the PinneDans association was established. Its goal was to develop brand-new contemporary patterns using entrelac, and to show the knitting world how fantastic this old technique could be, to prove that it's absolutely earned a place in today's knitting lexicon.

A Little History

What's so interesting about entrelac? Well, for one thing, it's a bit of a mystery. No sources can explain with certainty how or when entrelac was first developed. We do know it's quite an old technique. There are several theories about how it might have come to Norway; the most plausible is that the technique came with the Finns to Finnskogen. A Finnish group emigrating from Savolax came to Norway in the 1500-1600s, and brought with them particular skills and knowledge, including the art of birch bark weaving (*neverkontene*). Entrelac is very reminiscent of birch bark weaving, and the Norwegian term **kont**strikk is probably derived from *never**kont**ene*. Similarly, in Swedish, the technique is called **näver**stickning—based off a different part of the same word.

There is also a story concerning a Scottish ship lost along Norway's west coast; it's possible that survivors from that ship taught entrelac knitting to local people. What we do know is that entrelac has been found in several different parts of Norway, and that many people in each of these places believed it was a special local tradition.

Whatever its origins, entrelac has become known as a difficult knitting technique, and perhaps always has been. The knowledge was passed on from mother to daughter; and even in the old days, garments knitted with entrelac— for the most part, stockings—were more valuable than garments worked without. They were often considered particularly fine wear, and entrelac patterns are attested on several pairs of stockings made specifically for weddings. Knowledge of entrelac has been placed on the "red list" maintained by Norway's national handicrafts association, indicating that it is, in a manner of speaking, "endangered," and several local groups have chosen to make an effort to revive it.

Entrelac knitting can be found in multiple places in the world, but the Norwegian variation is special because the right side is always facing the knitter. That means you work in stockinette (stocking stitch) the whole time, without turning the work to purl. You work knit and purl stitches both to the left and to the right.

Entrelac gives a unique and striking look to garments, and with the fantastic choices available to knitters these days— different types of yarn, different colors or multicolored yarns, thick and thin yarns—the possibilities are endless. The blocks make the garments very elastic, and they're useful for shaping, too. Working entrelac also provides an excellent opportunity for using leftover yarns.

The Entrelac Technique

A Few Words Before You Begin

If you've never worked entrelac before, we have a few words of advice for you. Entrelac isn't as difficult as you might think, but there's a code you need to crack. Once that's done, you'll just need a little practice before you can knit with this technique.

Initially, most knitters will accidentally work more loosely than usual when knitting blocks. As a rule, practice will help with tension control. As in all knitting, gauge is important. Please read the section on gauge (see page 17) where you'll find some tips on how to measure gauge in entrelac knitting. Entrelac consists of blocks and tiers. You'll knit one block at a time, and when one block is complete, you start the next. A tier is a whole row of blocks, whether you knit in the round or back and forth. We recommend you begin with yarn and needles you're comfortable using.

Knitting with Right Side Always Facing

An important point with Norwegian entrelac is to always knit with the right side facing you throughout. This is, of course, not strictly necessary, but it makes the work considerably easier.

In all of our instructions, we assume as a given that the piece is worked in stockinette in both directions—from right to left, and from left to right. So the instructions won't include anything about turning the work or changing the direction of your knitting. Knitting stockinette back and forth, by turning the work and then purling over relatively few stitches, is tedious and takes longer. We recommend instead that you take up the challenge of learning how to knit in both directions so you can avoid turning the work. It's not as hard as you might think, and there are several ways of doing it. The most important thing is to find a method you like. We'll explain two methods for you:

Method 1:
Begin by holding the work as you usually do, with the yarn over the left index finger. Insert the left needle into the stitch on the right needle (point to point), and slip the stitch over to the left needle. Use the right needle to knit the stitch as usual. The new stitch is now on the right needle. Insert the left needle into the stitch from the right side of the front and slip it over to the left needle. When you slip the stitch from the right to left needle this way, you will twist the stitch into the correct position.

Method 2:
Begin by holding the work as you usually do, with the yarn over the left index finger. Insert the left needle into the stitch on the right needle (point to point), and slip the stitch from the right needle to the left needle. Use the right needle to lay the yarn over the left needle, and slip the stitch on the left needle over the yarn and off the needle. The stitch has now been knitted. A variation of this method is to use your left index finger to throw the yarn over the left needle instead of using the right needle.

Entrelac: Basic Principles

Entrelac consists of blocks. In order to knit the garments and designs included in this book, you'll begin with various types of blocks.
- Horizontal half blocks worked from left to right
- Horizontal half blocks worked from right to left
- Vertical blocks at the left side of the work
- Vertical half blocks at the right side of the work
- Whole blocks leaning from left to right
- Whole blocks leaning from right to left
- Quarter blocks at the left side of the work
- Quarter blocks at the right side of the work

In addition to knowing how to knit these various types of blocks, you'll need to learn how to increase and decrease within the blocks. But once you've mastered these elements, you'll be able to knit an endless number of entrelac variations.

Stitches align vertically in stockinette; but in entrelac, stitches lie on the diagonal. A vertical stitch takes up less room than a diagonal stitch. That means that you need fewer stitches to get the same width in entrelac as in stockinette. So you'll always need to decrease when shifting from stockinette to entrelac—and increase when shifting from entrelac to stockinette. A good rule of thumb is that every 3rd or 4th stitch should be decreased/increased, but this can vary depending on the yarn and the pattern. These calculations have been made for the patterns in this book, so you won't need to to worry about figuring it out yourself while knitting these designs.

A block is knitted back and forth over a specified number of stitches by working in stockinette—knit stitches—both towards the left and towards the right. For a neat result, you should always slip the first stitch on the needle.

When picking up and knitting stitches for a new block, always work through both loops of the stitch. Some books recommend that you work through only the back loop of the stitch; however, if you choose to pick up and knit only through one of the loops, then the work will be distinctly looser.

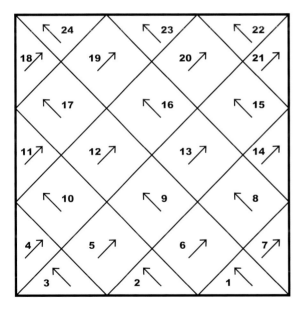

HORIZONTAL HALF BLOCKS AT BEGINNING OF PIECE

Blocks 1, 2, and 3 on schematic

When you want a straight edge at the beginning of the work in entrelac, or at the transition from stockinette to entrelac, begin with a row of horizontal half blocks.

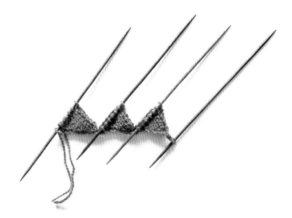

Row 1 (from left to right): K1.
Row 2 (from right to left): K1.
Row 3 (from left to right): Sl 1, k1.
Row 4 (from right to left): Sl 1, k1.
Row 5 (from left to right): Sl 1, k2.
Row 6 (from right to left): Sl 1, k2.

Repeat with 1 additional stitch every time you work towards the left, until the block has the required number of stitches. (Also work 2 rows back and forth after the last stitch in the block is knitted).

Sometimes, for example, on mittens or wrist warmers, you'll want the blocks to mirror-image each other on the right and left items. In that case, begin working the first row with horizontal half blocks towards the left on one piece and towards the right on the other one. If you are working flat, and you work the first row of half blocks from left to right, the methods for the vertical half blocks are reversed.

VERTICAL HALF BLOCKS AT LEFT SIDE OF PIECE

Block 4 on the schematic

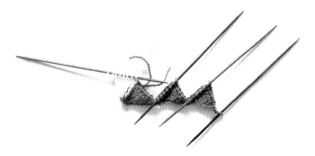

When you are knitting a square piece back and forth, a scarf, for example, you'll need to make vertical half blocks at each side of the item. As a general rule, you'll begin with 1 tier of horizontal half blocks. Normally, the instructions will specify that you have 1 edge stitch at each side of the piece. This edge stitch will be used when you knit the vertical half blocks. If an edge stitch is not included, cast on or pick up and knit 1 extra stitch before you begin the vertical half block. In some of the instructions, there will be several edge stitches; these are included in the cast-on number.

A vertical half block is worked by increasing inside the edge stitch and decreasing together with the block to the right (Block 3). Work as follows:

Row 1 (from left to right): Sl 1 (edge st), yo, k2tog (from Block 3).
Row 2 (from right to left): Work the yarnover as k1tbl, k1.
Row 3 (from left to right): Sl 1, yo, k1, k2tog.
Row 4 (from right to left): K1, work the yarnover as k1tbl, k1.

Repeat Rows 3-4, with 1 stitch more between the yarnover and the k2tog each time, until all the stitches are knitted together with those of the block to the right (Block 3). When the last 2 stitches have been knitted together, you'll be ready to begin the next block. Do not work 2 extra rows as for the horizontal half blocks.

WHOLE BLOCKS FROM LEFT TO RIGHT

Blocks 5 and 6 on the schematic

Working through both stitch loops, pick up and knit the required number of stitches for the block along the edge of the previous block (Block 3). Knit back and forth over these stitches. Begin by joining the last picked up stitch together with the first stitch in the block to the right (Block 2) = K2tog.

Now continue:
Row 1 (from right to left): Sl 1, k to end of needle.
Row 2 (from left to right): Sl 1, k to last st. Join last st to 1st st of block to right (block 2) = k2tog.

Rep Rows 1-2 until all the stitches in the block to the right (Block 2) have been joined to the new block (Block 5). Begin the next block (Block 6) immediately after the last 2 sts are joined.

VERTICAL HALF BLOCKS AT RIGHT SIDE OF PIECE

Block 7 on the schematic

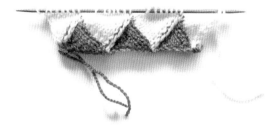

Working through both stitch loops, pick up and knit the required number of stitches for the block along the edge of the previous block (Block 1). The stitches are on the left needle. Work the edge stitch.

Now continue:

Row 1 (from right to left): Sl 1 (edge st), sl 1, k1, psso, knit to end of row.

Row 2 (from left to right): Sl 1, k to end of row.

Rep Rows 1-2 until 2 sts remain on needle (1 edge st + 1 st). The 2nd st becomes the 1st st on the next block. The edge stitch should rest until the next time you knit a vertical half block on the right side of the work.

WHOLE BLOCKS FROM LEFT TO RIGHT

Blocks 8, 9, and 10 on the schematic

Working through both stitch loops, pick up and knit the required number of stitches for the block along the edge of the previous block (Block 7). Knit back and forth over these stitches. Begin by knitting the last stitch picked up together with the first stitch on the block to the left (Block 6) as follows: sl 1, k1, psso.

Now continue:

Row 1 (from left to right): Sl 1, knit to end of row.

Row 2 (from right to left): Sl 1, knit to last st. Join last st to 1st st of block to right (block 6) = sl 1, k1, psso.

Row 3 (from left to right): Sl 1, knit to end of row.

Rep Rows 2-3 until all the stitches in the block to the left (Block 6) have been joined to the new block (Block 8). Begin the next block (Block 9) immediately after the last 2 sts are joined.

Continue, working Blocks 11-21 following the schematic.

HORIZONTAL HALF BLOCKS AT END OF PIECE

Blocks 22, 23, and 24 on the schematic

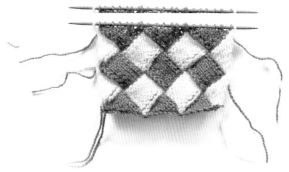

Working through both stitch loops, pick up and knit stitches for the block along the block to the right (Block 21). Begin by working the last stitch picked up together with the first stitch of the block to the left (Block 20) as follows: sl 1, k1, psso.

Now continue:

Row 1 (from left to right): Sl 1, knit until 1 st remains of the picked-up sts.

Row 2 (from right to left): Sl 1, knit to last st. Join last st to 1st st of block to right = sl 1, k1, psso.

Row 3 (from left to right): Sl 1, knit to end of row but with 1 st fewer than on Row 1.

Repeat Rows 2-3, with 1 stitch fewer each time you knit towards the right, until you've joined all the stitches from Block 22 together with the stitches of the block to the left (Block 20). Begin the next block (Block 23) immediately after the last two stitches have been joined.

Knitting Tip: When you are counting but unsure of how many stitches you should knit towards the left before you change the direction of the knitting, count the number of stitches on the right needle. That's the number of stitches you should knit towards the left, including the stitch you will join with the block to the right.

QUARTER BLOCKS

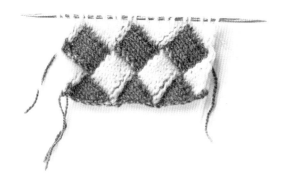

Sometimes, quarter blocks are needed to fill out a pattern. These blocks are constructed differently for the right and left sides of the work.

QUARTER BLOCK ON THE LEFT SIDE OF PIECE

The first part of a quarter block is worked as for a vertical half block on the left side of the work.

Work as follows:
Row 1 (from left to right): Sl 1 (edge st, yo, k2tog.
Row 2 (from right to left): Knit the yarnover tbl, k1.
Row 3 (from left to right): Sl 1 (edge st), yo, k2tog.
Row 4 (from right to left): K1, k1tbl (through yarnover of previous row).

Repeat Rows 3-4, with 1 st more between the yarnover and the k2tog each time until you reach half the total number of stitches needed for the block. End on the right side of the block.

Continue constructing the block as for a horizontal half block to the end of the piece.
Row 1 (from right to left): Sl 1, knit until 1 st rem.
Row 2 (from left to right): Sl 1, knit to last st, k2tog with last st and 1st st of block to the right.
Row 3 (from right to left): Sl 1, knit towards the left until 2 sts rem.
Row 4 (from left to right): Sl 1, knit to last st; k2tog with last st and 1st st of block to the right.

Repeat Rows 3-4 until all the sts of the block to the right have been joined to the quarter block.

QUARTER BLOCK ON THE RIGHT SIDE OF PIECE

This block is worked as for both the vertical half block for right side of work, and *at the same time* as a horizontal half block at the end of a piece.

Working through both loops, pick up and knit the required number of stitches along the edge of the previous block. The stitches should be on the left needle. Work edge stitches.

Row 1 (from right to left): Sl 1 (edge st), sl 1, k1, psso, knit until 1 st rem.
Row 2 (from left to right): Sl 1, knit to end of row.
Row 3 (from right to left): Sl 1, sl 1, k1, psso, knit until 2 sts rem.

Repeat Rows 2-3, knitting 1 stitch fewer to the left for every row until 1 stitch remains.

Knitting in the Round

Many of the garments in this book are knitted in the round. In those instances, the vertical half blocks are not worked as for those shown on the schematic. There will be half blocks only in the first and last horizontal tiers, while the rest of the tiers consist only of whole blocks. The new blocks are joined with a block from the previous tier. The tiers are worked, alternately, from right to left on one tier and from left to right on the next tier.

Increasing and Decreasing within Blocks

In order to shape a garment, or, for example, to knit a round yoke sweater, you need to learn how to increase or decrease from one tier to the next. The increases and decreases are made within the blocks.

INCREASING

When knitting a new block, you increase both in the new block and in the block the new one is joined to. The increases should be evenly spaced in the block you are joining the new one to. Decide ahead of time how to space the increases. Pick up and knit stitches through both loops at the same time as you make one (M1) for each extra stitch to be added. Space the increases evenly across. So the block will be square, add an extra row for every new stitch added (every M1).

When knitting blocks from right to left:
As you join to the block to the left, increase by picking up the strand between 2 stitches in the block you will join to the new block. Join the blocks by knitting the new stitch and then passing over the stitch from the right block. Increase evenly spaced along the block.

When knitting blocks from left to right:
As you join to a block to the right, increase by picking up the strand between 2 stitches in the block you will join to the new block. In this case, twist the strand (as for a twisted yarnover) before you knit the stitch from the left block immediately together with the twisted stitch from the block to the right. Increase evenly spaced along the block.

DECREASING

When decreasing stitches from one block to another, pick up and knit the required number of stitches that the new block needs at the beginning of the block. When you join it to the block at its side, knit 1 stitch from the new block together with 2 stitches from the previous block = 3 stitches knitted together. Repeat this decrease as many times as the number of stitches to be decreased.

If you want to have a lesser rate of increase/decrease per row, for example, on knee socks or sleeves, decrease/increase only by picking up and knitting fewer/more stitches for the new block without decreasing/increasing in the block you are joining it to, so you will have the same total number of rows. Each decrease/increase will be over two rows.

"Star" Shaping

Hats, mittens, and sock toes are formed with "star" shaping on the last tier of the piece.

Instructions: Work the first block as for a regular whole block, whether it is knit to the right or left. The rest of the blocks are also worked as whole blocks but you will join each to the blocks on both sides of the new block. Use the same method as when knitting whole blocks (= k2tog on the right side and sl 1, k1, psso on the left side). Work a row over all the stitches in the block to end at the place where you would pick up and knit stitches for a new block. When all the blocks are knitted this way, you will only have the stitches from the last block on the needle. Bind off remaining stitches. Sew or Kitchener stitch the first and last blocks together. Insert the yarn into the edge of the work and tighten. Cut yarns and weave in on wrong side.

Knitting with Two Colors

When knitting with two colors, 1 tier of each color, knit as follows to avoid cutting and re-attaching the yarn for each color change: Knit 1 extra row on the last block, up at the top of the block. Now the yarn is ready to begin with on the next block of that color. When working with two colors, the beginning of the tiers will shift diagonally.

Avoiding "Holes" in the Transition Between Entrelac and Stockinette

Holes can develop in the transition between entrelac and stockinette. The problem is most noticeable when you go from entrelac to stockinette. To avoid holes, pick up a new stitch (= M1) between each of the stitches in the half blocks on the first round (when knitting over all the stitches) after the entrelac knitting. On the next round, reduce the stitch count to the specified count given in the instructions. This takes a little effort but the result will be a smooth and tight transition. You won't have to do this every time; when we feel it's necessary for a nice-looking transition, we will indicate that in the garment instructions.

Two-End Knitting (Twined Knitting)

Two-end knitting (also called twined knitting) has a long history, both in Norway and around the world. As the name implies, two-end knitting is worked with two strands of yarn, alternating between strands. For both knitting and purling, the yarns twist between the stitches each time they change places in the sequence. You can create patterns by varying the sequence of knit and purl stitches and the way the strands twist around each other. Two-end knitting makes a firm, thick fabric, so it's often used for mittens.

Two-end knitting has also been used in combination with entrelac, particularly for the cast-on. A few rounds of two-end knitting before entrelac on mittens, for example, add a lovely decorative touch. In some places, a two-end purl braid is referred to as a "Latvian" braid.

Here's how to make a two-end purl braid:

We used two colors for our sample.
Color 1: Red.
Color 2: White.

Rnd 1: (K1 Color 1, k1 Color 2) around.
Rnd 2: Bring both colors to the front of the work and hold both on the front throughout. When changing colors, always bring the new color OVER the old one. This makes the strands twist on every stitch, but they will untwist on the next round. (P1 Color 1, p1 Color 2) around.
Rnd 3: Bring both colors to the front of the work and hold both on the front throughout. When changing colors, always bring the new color UNDER the old one. (P1 Color 1, p1 Color 2) around.

If you want to reverse the direction of the braid on the second mitten, work Rnd 1, then reverse Rnds 2 and 3 (that is, work Rnd 3 and then Rnd 2).

Elastic Cast-On

You'll need a good and elastic cast-on for entrelac. An entrelac stitch, which lies on the diagonal, takes up more space than a stockinette stitch. So a regular cast-on method will be too firm and tight for entrelac stitches.

Knitted Cast-On:
Make a slip knot loop and place it on the left needle. Hold the needle for knitting as usual. Insert the right needle into the loop; knit 1 loose stitch, twisting that stitch as you place it on the left needle; tighten slightly. Make a new loose stitch exactly the same way, twisting it as you place it on the left needle. Continue the same way until you have the required number of stitches. Make sure you don't tighten the stitches too much or the cast-on will be too tight. There are a number of other ways to cast on loosely—check the internet for various methods.

I-Cord Bind-Off

Some of the garments in this book use an I-cord bind-off as a lovely and very suitable edging for entrelac knitting.

I-Cord Instructions:
When you are ready to bind off at the beginning of a round, cast on 3 new sts.

K2, k2tog tbl. Now there are 3 sts on the right needle. Slip all 3 sts back to left needle. Rep from * to * until 3 sts rem on the round. Now k2tog, slip sts from right to left needle, knit last 2 sts together.

Knitting in General

KNITTING GAUGE (TENSION)

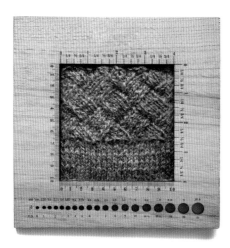

Every pattern lists the knitting gauge and finished garment measurements. As we mentioned previously, gauge is a bit tricky to measure with entrelac.

In stockinette, you usually knit a gauge swatch a minimum of 4 x 4 in / 10 x 10 cm and count the number of stitches in 4 in / 10 cm across the width and up the length. If the number of stitches and rows in 4 in / 10 cm doesn't match the numbers given in the pattern, you need to try another needle size.

So, what do you do with entrelac? The method we recommend is: first knit a gauge swatch in stockinette and then decrease every 3rd stitch over a row. Before you begin the entrelac, count the number of stitches in 4 in / 10 cm. If they match the recommended gauge, proceed with the entrelac. Knit a round of horizontal half blocks with, for example, 6 or 7 stitches; work 2 tiers of whole blocks + vertical half blocks at each side. Add a tier of horizontal half blocks. Finally, knit 1 round in stockinette, increasing the stitch count to match the original cast-on.

If the gauges for the stockinette and entrelac sections match, your swatch should have smooth knit edges. If you've knitted the entrelac more loosely than the stockinette, the entrelac section will be wider than the stockinette. In that case, go down a needle size when working in entrelac. On the other hand, if the entrelac is tighter than the stockinette, go up a needle size.

It can be awfully tiresome to knit a gauge swatch, but it's even more tiresome to knit a whole sweater that doesn't fit.

These mittens were knitted with exactly the same stitch count and number of rows. The smaller one was worked with very fine yarn and small needles (U. S. size 000 / 1.5 mm) and the larger one with heavier yarn and bigger needles (U. S. size 6 / 4 mm). They are a good illustration of the importance of correct gauge.

INCREASING AND DECREASING

There are various ways to decrease stitches. If, for example, the instructions say to decrease every 4th stitch, it means that you work 2 stitches and then join the next 2. To decrease every 3rd stitch, work 1 stitch and then join the next 2.

In other instances, it might simply say to decrease evenly spaced across or around, which means that you have to calculate the spacing of the decreases. If you have 40 stitches and need to decrease down to 30 stitches, first figure out how many stitches must be eliminated: 40 - 30 = 10. Now divide the original number of stitches by the number to decrease to determine how often to decrease: 40/10 = 4. So, you should decrease every 4th stitch.

You can calculate increases the same way. If there are 30 stitches and you need to increase to 40: 40 - 30 = 10; 30/10 = 3. So, (knit 3 and then increase 1) 10 times.

There are various methods for decreasing and increasing. It's standard to decrease with knit 2 together, either as regular knit sts (k2tog) or twisted (k2tog tbl). Another method is to slip 1, knit 1, pass slipped st over (sl 1, k1, psso).

An easy increase is a yarnover, which is knitted through the back loop on the next row or round. Another common method is a make 1 (M1): lift the strand between two stitches and knit into back loop.

Yarnover

To make a yarnover, bring the yarn loosely over the needle from the front of the needle on the right side to the back of the needle on the left side, when working from right to left. If you are working across from left to right, bring the yarn from the back of the needle on the left side to the front of the needle on the right side.

Tools

Wood needles are better than metal ones for entrelac. Metal needles are heavier and smoother and can easily slide out of the stitches. Needles with sharp points make it easier to pick up and knit stitches along the edge of a block. If you find it difficult to pick up stitches, you can use a crochet hook instead. Insert the hook through both stitch loops, catch the yarn, and transfer the stitch to the knitting needle (making sure the stitch is sitting correctly on the needle). Double-pointed knitting needles 6 in / 15 cm long are easier to handle than needles 8 in / 20 cm long.

Abbreviations

BO	bind off (UK cast off)	rem	remain(s)(ing)
cm	centimeter(s)	rep	repeat
CO	cast on	RS	right side
dpn	double-pointed needles	sl	slip
		sl m	slip marker
est	established; that is, continue in pattern	ssk	(sl 1 knitwise) 2 times, insert left needle left to right through the 2 sts and knit together through back loops = left-leaning decrease
in	inch(es)		
k	knit		
k2tog	knit 2 together = right-leaning decrease		
m	meter(s)		
M1	make 1 = with needle tip, from front to back, pick up strand between 2 sts and knit into back loop = left-leaning increase	st(s)	stitch(es)
		St st	stockinette (UK stocking stitch)
		tbl	through back loop(s)
		WS	wrong side
		yd	yard(s)
		yo	yarnover
pm	place marker		
psso	pass slipped stitch over		

> "Always make it a rule to read entirely through the pattern instructions before you start to knit. Also check the knitting guidelines on this page and follow the tips we offer. Knitting will then be a sport rather than toil."
>
> *ALLE KVINNER STRIKKER [ALL WOMEN KNIT], 1953 (VINTAGESTRIKK [VINTAGE KNITTING], 2013)*

Entrelac Knits for Beginners

In this chapter, we've collected a few patterns perfect for beginners. Our best advice is to start with a small project, use needles and yarn you are comfortable with, and knit something you find tempting. If you want to begin with a larger project, though, don't let anything hold you back.

Take some time to "crack the code" and practice. There's no reason to hesitate, just jump right in. Many knitters are surprised at how easy entrelac actually is.

Petunia

HEADBAND

A simple headband—perfect
for beginners. Knit it with two
colors for a pretty effect. Of
course, you can knit it with only
one color, too, if you like, or
with several. It's a great little
project for using up leftover
yarns.

SKILL LEVEL: Experienced
SIZE: Approx. 21¾-23¾ in / 55-60 cm circumference
MATERIALS
Yarn:
   CYCA #3 (DK, light worsted) Smart from
   Sandnes (100% wool, 109 yd/100 m / 50 g)
Yarn Colors and Amounts:
   Blue 5936: 50 g
   Light Blue 5904: 50 g
Needles:
   U. S. size 4 / 3.5 mm: short circular
GAUGE
21 sts in St st = 4 in / 10 cm.
Adjust needle size to obtain correct gauge
if necessary.

The headband is knitted in the round and consists of 12 blocks with 7 sts in each block. It begins and ends with rolled edges.

With Light Blue, CO 96 sts. Join, being careful not to twist cast-on row. Knit 7 rnds. On the next rnd, decrease evenly spaced around to 84 sts. Now begin working in entrelac. Make a tier of 12 horizontal half blocks, leaning from right to left. Change to Blue and make a tier with 12 whole blocks leaning from left to right. Change to Light Blue and make a tier of 12 whole blocks leaning from right to left. Change to Blue to make 12 whole blocks leaning from left to right. Change back to Light Blue and work 12 horizontal half blocks leaning from right to left. Knit 1 rnd over all the sts, and, *at the same time*, increase evenly spaced around to 96 sts. Knit 7 rnds. BO loosely. Cut yarn and weave in all ends neatly on WS.

Turøy

Turøy is an island off the west coast of Norway. A hat, scarf, and wrist warmers form the Turøy set, knitted with Rauma's Puno, a lovely, soft, light yarn. The result is an attractive set that looks good on everyone.

The hat comes in two sizes. We attached a fake fur pompom with a snap to make washing easier. The scarf is worked back and forth. If you want a scarf longer than the one described in the instructions, don't forget to buy extra yarn. The fine, soft wrist warmers feature thumb openings.

HAT

SKILL LEVEL: Experienced
SIZES: M (L)
MATERIALS
Yarn:
    CYCA #5 (bulky) Puno from Rauma (68% alpaca, 22% nylon, 10% Merino wool, 120 yd/110 m / 50 g)
Yarn Color and Amount:
    White 811 or Light Gray 1310: 50 (100) g
Other Materials:
    1 fake fur pompom with a snap attachment
Needles:
U. S. size 8 / 5 mm: circular
GAUGE
18 sts in St st = 4 in / 10 cm.
Adjust needle size to obtain correct gauge if necessary.

_____

CO 72 (80) sts. Join, being careful not to twist cast-on row; pm for beginning of rnd. Work 10 rnds k2, p2 ribbing. Knit 1 rnd, *at the same time* decreasing evenly spaced around to 60 (70) sts. Now work entrelac in the round: Work 1 tier with 10 horizontal half blocks leaning from right to left, with 6 (7) sts in each block. Next, work 4 (5) tiers with whole blocks changing block direction on each tier. End with a "star" shaping (see page 15). Cut yarn and weave in ends neatly on WS. Attach a pompom.

SCARF

SKILL LEVEL: Experienced
SIZE: One size
FINISHED MEASUREMENTS
Approx. 9½ x 71 in / 24 x 180 cm
MATERIALS
Yarn:
    CYCA #5 (bulky) Puno from Rauma (68% alpaca, 22% nylon, 10% Merino wool, 120 yd/110 m / 50 g)
Yarn Color and Amount:
    White 811 or Light Gray 1310: 250 g (buy more yarn if you decide to lengthen scarf)
Needles:
    U. S. size 8 / 5 mm: circular
GAUGE
18 sts in St st = 4 in / 10 cm.
Adjust needle size to obtain correct gauge if necessary.

_____

CO 28 sts with an elastic cast-on method (see page 16 for Knitted CO). Make sure the cast-on edge is not too tight. Work 1 tier with 4 horizontal half blocks leaning from right to left, with 7 sts in each block. Work 1 vertical half block at the left side of the scarf, and then 3 whole blocks from left to right, before ending the tier with 1 vertical half block at the right side of scarf. On the next tier, work 4 whole blocks leaning from right to left. Repeat these 2 tiers until scarf is approx. 71 in / 180 cm long or desired length. Work 1 tier of horizontal half blocks. BO loosely; cut yarn and weave in ends neatly on WS.

WRIST WARMERS

SKILL LEVEL: Experienced
SIZE: One size
FINISHED MEASUREMENTS
Length 8¼ in / 21 cm
MATERIALS
Yarn:
    CYCA #5 (bulky) Puno from Rauma (68% alpaca, 22% nylon, 10% Merino wool, 120 yd/110 m / 50 g)
Yarn Colors and Amounts:
    White 811 or Light Gray 1310: 50 g
Needles:
    U. S. size 8 / 5 mm: circular
GAUGE
18 sts in St st = 4 in / 10 cm.
Adjust needle size to obtain correct gauge if necessary.

Right-Hand Wrist Warmer
CO 25 sts with an elastic cast-on method (see page 16 for Knitted CO). Join to work in the round. Work 1 tier with 5 horizontal half blocks leaning from right to left, with 5 sts in each block. Now work 5 tiers of whole blocks, changing block direction each tier. On Tier 6, make the thumbhole: BO the sts of the last block. On the last block of Tier 7, do not join with a block from Tier 6. Work 2 tiers of whole blocks and then 1 tier of horizontal half blocks. BO loosely.

Left-Hand Wrist Warmer
Work as for right hand, but mirror-image. Begin by working the first tier from left to right.

WEARING WHAT YOU'VE MADE

" This can be the most fun: to show off some funky scarf that reveals your inner cool. And other times it's just so hard to wear something that seems less than perfect or didn't turn out the way you wanted it to. But just put it on anyway; celebrate your hard work and your talent. And your love. Every knitter stitches with love, even when they're just starting, all red-faced and frustrated. Why else would we create? Especially in a world that doesn't need homemade anything. That's when we need homemade everything. It never matters if things don't end up just the way you planned. Every moment is a work in progress; every stitch is one stitch closer. There may be worse, but there is always better. When you wear something you've made with your own hands, you surround yourself with love, and all the love that came before you. The real achievement, you see, is being proud of what you've made. I know that I am. "

KATE JACOBS,
THE FRIDAY NIGHT KNITTING CLUB
(G. P. PUTNAM'S SONS, 2007)

Accessories

Traditionally, entrelac was used for mittens and socks, and it's just as pretty now as it was then. But, there are so many other projects entrelac is perfect for. These small garments and accessories are both practical and lovely—great as gifts for anyone, including yourself. By varying the thickness of the yarn, and changing the yarn quality, colors, and block size, you create an ocean full of possibilities.

Røst

Røst is an island municipality in Nordland, in the far north of Norway. These wrist warmers have rolled edges at each end, and no thumb openings. The sizes are adjusted by the gauge. For small hands, work with needles U. S. size 1.5 / 2.5 mm and, for larger hands, try U. S. size 2.5 / 3 mm. The wrist warmers are knitted with space-dyed yarns for a special look, and the cuffs in a pair will not be identical. They may look fairly different, depending on where you start in the color sequence.

EASY WRIST WARMERS WITH ROLLED EDGES

SKILL LEVEL: Experienced
SIZE: Women's
FINISHED MEASUREMENTS
Length: 5½ (6¾, 8¼) in / 14 (17, 21) cm
Circumference: 8¼ in / 21 cm on needles U. S. size
   1.5 / 2.5 mm or 9½ in / 24 cm on needles U. S.
   2.5 / 3 mm
MATERIALS
Yarn:
   CYCA #1 (fingering) Drops Delight from Garnstudio
   (75% wool, 25% nylon, 191 yd/175 m / 50 g)
Yarn Colors and Amounts:
   Raspberry Cake 17: 50 g
   Alternate Color 1: Plum/Beige/Heather 02
   Alternate Color 2: Green/Blue 16
Needles:
   U. S. size 1.5 (small) or 2.5 (large) / 2.5 or 3 mm:
   set of 5 dpn
GAUGE
Large size: 23 sts in St st = 4 in / 10 cm.
Small size: 26 sts in St st = 4 in / 10 cm.
Adjust needle size to obtain correct gauge if necessary.

CO 56 sts. Divide the sts evenly onto 4 dpn and join to work in the round. Knit 8 rnds. Next, knit 1 rnd, *at the same time* decreasing every 4th st evenly spaced around = 42 sts rem. Now work entrelac in the round. Begin with 1 tier of 6 horizontal half blocks leaning from right to left, with 7 sts in each block. Work 7 (9, 11) tiers of whole blocks, alternating tiers with blocks leaning from left to right and from right to left. Work 1 tier of horizontal half blocks. Knit 1 rnd over all the sts, *at the same time* increasing evenly spaced around to 56 sts. Knit 8 rnds in St st as for the beginning of the cuff. BO loosely.

Knit the second wrist warmer the same way. Weave in all ends neatly on WS.

Mittens for Everyone

Traditionally, mittens have been a popular project for entrelac knitting, making it a "must" in our book. The inspiration of new yarns and the need to test out various qualities led to several different patterns. We've made both mittens with entrelac only on the cuffs, and mittens with entrelac all over.

Vilje

WOMEN'S MITTENS
Vilje is a Norwegian first name.
These are easy women's mittens,
with entrelac on the cuffs and ribbing
between the mitten hand and cuff to
help make the mittens fit well.

SKILL LEVEL: Experienced
SIZE: Women's

MATERIALS
Yarn:
    CYCA #3 (DK, light worsted) Mitu from Rauma (50%
    wool, 50% alpaca, 109 yd/100 m / 50 g) OR Drops
    Lima from Garnstudio (65% wool, 35% alpaca,
    109 yd/100 m / 50 g)
Yarn Color and Amount:
    White SFN10 or Gray Heather SFN13: 100 g
Needles:
    U.S. size 6 / 4 mm: set of 5 dpn
GAUGE
21 sts in St st = 4 in / 10 cm.
Adjust needle size to obtain correct gauge if
necessary.

_____

Both Mittens

CO 40 sts and divide sts evenly onto dpn. Join and
knit 8 rnds. Knit 1 rnd, decreasing every 4th st = 30
sts rem. Now work entrelac in the round. Work 1
tier of 6 horizontal half blocks that lean from right to
left, with 5 sts in each block. Continue with 3 tiers of
whole blocks, alternating block direction in each tier.
Knit 1 tier of horizontal half blocks.
Knit 1 rnd, increasing evenly spaced around to 40 sts.
Work 6 rnds k1tbl, p1 ribbing.

Left-Hand Mitten

Continue in St st. On the 2nd rnd after the ribbing,
begin increasing for the thumb gusset as follows:
Increase Rnd 1: Increase with yo at each side of
the next-to-last st of rnd, k1. Pm before/after each
yarnover.
Knit 2 rnds; throughout gusset, on following rnd, knit
each yarnover as k1tbl.
Increase Rnd 2: Knit to marker, sl m, yo, k3, yo, sl m.
Knit 2 rnds.
Increase Rnd 3: Knit to marker, sl m, yo, k5, yo, sl m,
k1.
On every 3rd rnd, increase the same way within
markers until there are 9 sts between the markers.
Knit 3 rnds. Now place the thumb sts + 1 st on each
side = 11 sts total, on a holder. CO 3 new sts over the
gap. Continue in St st for 3¼ in / 8 cm or to desired
length before top shaping (or at top of little finger).

Top Shaping: Divide the sts evenly (10 sts on
each needle) onto 4 dpn; the rnd begins on Ndl 2.
Decrease on every rnd as follows:
Ndls 1 and 3: K7, k2tog, k1.
Ndls 2 and 4: K1, ssk or sl 1, k1, psso, k7.
Decrease the same way, with 1 st fewer per needle
on each rnd, until 8 sts total remain. Cut yarn and
draw end through rem 8 sts; tighten.

Thumb: Place held sts of thumb gusset onto dpn
and pick up and knit 5 sts along top of thumbhole =
16 sts total. Knit around in St st until thumb measures
approx. 2¼ in / 5.5 cm. Shape top by repeating
(k2tog) around and around until 8 sts rem. Cut yarn
and draw end through rem sts; tighten.

Right-Hand Mitten

Work as for left mitten, reversing placement of
thumb = begin increasing on the 2nd st of the rnd.

Idun

CHILDREN'S MITTENS
Idun is the name of a Norse goddess. These mittens will fit children well, with entrelac on the cuffs and ribbing between the mitten hand and cuff.

CHILDREN'S MITTENS

SKILL LEVEL: Experienced
SIZES: Children's sizes 2/4 (5/7, 8/10) years
MATERIALS
Yarn:
   CYCA #1 (fingering) Inca from Rauma (100% alpaca,
   191 yd/175 m / 50 g)
Yarn Color and Amount:
   Color 776: 50 g
Needles:
   U.S. size 1.5 / 2.5 mm: set of 5 dpn
GAUGE
26 sts in St st = 4 in / 10 cm;
Adjust needle size to obtain correct gauge if
necessary.

_____

Both Mittens
CO 40 (48, 48) sts and divide sts evenly onto dpn.
Join and knit 8 rnds. Knit 1 rnd, decreasing every
4th st = 30 (36, 36) sts rem. Now work entrelac in
the round. Make 1 tier with 6 horizontal half blocks
that lean from right to left, with 5 (6, 6) sts in each
block. Continue with 3 (3, 4) tiers of whole blocks,
alternating the block direction in each tier. Knit 1 tier
of horizontal half blocks.
Sizes 2/4 and 5/7: Work 6 rnds k1tbl, p1 ribbing.
Size 8/10: Knit 1 rnd, increasing evenly spaced
around to 48 sts. Work 6 rnds k1tbl, p1 ribbing.
All sizes: After completing ribbing, knit 1 rnd,
increasing evenly spaced around to 40 (48, 56) sts.

Left-Hand Mitten
Continue in St st. On the 2nd rnd after the ribbing,
begin increasing for the thumb gusset as follows:
Increase Rnd 1: Increase with yo at each side of
the next-to-last st of rnd, k1. Pm before/after each
yarnover.
Knit 2 rnds; throughout gusset, on following rnd, knit
each yarnover as k1tbl.
Increase Rnd 2: Knit to marker, sl m, yo, k3, yo, sl m.
Knit 2 rnds.
Increase Rnd 3: Knit to marker, sl m, yo, k5, yo, sl
m, k1.
On every 3rd rnd, increase the same way within
markers a total of 3 (4, 5) times = 7 (9, 11) thumb
sts, between the markers.
Knit 3 rnds. Now place the thumb sts + 1 st on each

side (= 9, 11, 13) sts on a holder. CO 3 new sts over
the gap. Continue in St st for 2¼ (2½, 3) in / 5.5 (6.5,
7.5) cm or to desired length before top shaping (or at
top of little finger).

Top Shaping: Divide the sts evenly onto 4 dpn [10
(12, 14) sts on each needle]; the rnd begins on Ndl 2.
Decrease on every rnd as follows:
Ndls 1 and 3: K7 (9, 11), k2tog, k1.
Ndls 2 and 4: K1, ssk or sl 1, k1, psso, k7 (9, 11).
Decrease the same way, with 1 st fewer per needle
on each rnd, until 8 sts total remain. Cut yarn and
draw end through rem 8 sts; tighten.

Thumb: Place held sts of thumb gusset onto dpn
and pick up and knit 3 sts along top of thumbhole =
12 (14, 16) sts total. Knit around in St st until thumb
measures approx. 1½ (2, 2¼) in / in / 4 (5, 6) cm.
Shape top by repeating (k2tog) around and around
until 8 sts rem. Cut yarn and draw end through rem
sts; tighten.

Right-Hand Mitten
Work as for left mitten, reversing placement of
thumb = begin increasing on the 2nd st of the rnd.

Block Mittens

Traditional mittens beginning with a two-end
purl braid and then entrelac diamonds
all over.

SKILL LEVEL: Experienced
SIZES: Women's (men's)
MATERIALS
Yarn:
  CYCA #1 (fingering) Finull PT2 from Rauma
  (100% wool, 191 yd/175 m / 50 g)
Yarn Colors and Amounts:
  Color 1: Gray Heather 404-x (Light Grey Heather
  403-x): 100 g
  Color 2: Natural 401-x (Dark Gray Heather 405-x):
  100 g
Needles:
  U.S. size 1.5 / 2.5 mm: set of 5 dpn
GAUGE
26 sts in St st = 4 in / 10 cm.
Adjust needle size to obtain correct gauge if
necessary.

_____

Both Mittens

With Color 1, CO 84 (98) sts and divide sts evenly
onto dpn. Join and work a two-end purl braid
(see page 16). If you want the braid to point in the
opposite direction on the second mitten, reverse
braid Rnds 2 and 3. Knit 1 rnd.

Right-Hand Mitten

Tier 1: With Color 1, work whole blocks from right
to left.

Row 1 (from right to left): Sl 1, k5 (6), ssk or sl 1,
k1, psso.
Row 2 (from left to right): Sl 1, knit to end of row.

Rep Rows 1-2 a total of 5 (6) times. Work Row 1
once more. You now have a whole block with 6 (7)
sts. Continue with the next whole block until there
are 7 whole blocks around.

Continue with whole blocks, alternating colors in
each tier and alternating tiers to the left and right
until there are 9 tiers of whole blocks.

Next tier (Tier 10), work as follows:
Work 4 whole blocks.
Block 5: Pick up and knit 6 (7) sts. Work back and
forth over these sts without joining to the block from
the previous tier until you've worked 12 (14) rows.
Place the next 2 blocks of the previous tier on a
holder for the thumb.

Block 6: CO 6 (7) new sts. Work back and forth over
these sts, _at the same time_ joining them with the last
block of previous tier.
Starting with Tier 6, there are only 6 blocks around.
Continue in entrelac around with whole blocks until
there are a total of 15 (16) tiers.

End with the "star" shaping (see page 15). Cut yarn
and fasten off.

Thumb: Pick up and knit 6 (7) sts in the cast-on edge
for the new block on Tier 10. Pick up and knit 6 (7)
sts along the side of the next-to-last block on Tier
10. Work 1 whole block over the last 6 (7) sts that
were picked up, and join the block to the first 6 (7)
sts picked up. Place the held sts on the needle = 3
blocks for the thumb. Work around in entrelac until
you have 3 tiers of whole blocks. Shape top of thumb
as for top of mitten.

Left-Hand Mitten

Work as for right-hand mitten, reversing placement
of thumb.

Frøya

Frøya is the Norwegian name for a Nordic goddess of love. This elegant set includes women's gloves and a tam. If you want to knit a version for a man, make it with somewhat heavier yarn and bigger needles and it'll turn out larger. The hat is worked from the top down.

GLOVES

SKILL LEVEL: Experienced
SIZES: Women's S/M (M/L)
MATERIALS
Yarn:
CYCA #1 (fingering) Sølje from Hillesvåg (100% Norwegian wool, 383 yd/350 m / 100 g)
Yarn Color and Amount:
Cognac 642103: 100 g
Needles:
U.S. size 1.5 / 2.5 mm: set of 5 dpn
GAUGE
25 sts in St st = 4 in / 10 cm.
Adjust needle size to obtain correct gauge if necessary.

_____

Left-Hand Glove
CO 56 (56) sts and divide evenly onto 4 dpn. Join and knit 8 rnds. Knit 1 rnd, decreasing evenly spaced around to 42 (42) sts (= eliminate every 4th st). Now work entrelac in the round. Work 1 tier of 6 horizontal half block that lean from right to left, with 7 sts in each block. Continue with 5 tiers of whole blocks, changing direction of blocks each tier. Work 1 tier of horizontal half blocks. There should be 42 sts around. Now change to St st. On the first rnd, increase evenly spaced around to 48 (56) sts. Take measurements from this round. After ⅜ in / 1 cm, begin increasing for the thumb gusset.

Work the gusset as follows:
Increase Rnd 1: Increase with yo at each side of the next-to-last st of rnd, k1. Pm before/after each yarnover.
Knit 2 rnds; throughout gusset, on following rnd, knit each yarnover as k1tbl.

Increase Rnd 2: Knit to marker, sl m, yo, k3, yo, sl m. Knit 2 rnds.
Increase Rnd 3: Knit to marker, sl m, yo, k5, yo, sl m, k1.
On every 3rd rnd, increase the same way within markers a total of 5 (6) times = 11 (13) thumb sts between the markers. Continue in St st until glove measures 2½ (2¾) in / 6 (7) cm above entrelac. Now place the thumb sts + 1 st at each side—a total of 13 (15) sts—on a holder. CO 3 new sts over gap. Continue around in St st until glove measures 3½ (4¼) in / 9 (11) cm above entrelac. Divide sts onto two holders with the sts of Ndls 1 and 2 on one holder and sts on Ndls 3 and 4 on the other holder. The round begins with Ndl 1.

Index Finger: Pick up and knit 7 (8) sts from each holder and CO 2 new sts at base of middle finger = 16 (18) sts total. Work around in St st for approx. 2½ (3) in / 6.5 (7.5) cm. Shape fingertip with k2tog around until 8 sts rem. Cut yarn and draw end through rem sts; tighten.

Middle Finger: Pick up and knit 6 (7) sts from each holder, pick up and knit 2 new sts at base of index finger, CO 1 st at ring finger = 15 (17) sts total. Work around in St st for approx. 3 (3¼) in / 7.5 (8.5) cm. Shape fingertip with k2tog around until 8 sts rem. Cut yarn and draw end through rem sts; tighten.

Ring Finger: Pick up and knit 6 (7) sts from each holder, pick up and knit 1 new st at base of middle finger and CO 1 st at little finger = 14 (16) sts total. Work around in St st for approx. 2¾ (3) in / 7 (8) cm. Shape fingertip with k2tog around until 8 sts rem. Cut yarn and draw end through rem sts; tighten.

Little Finger: Pick up and knit 5 (6) sts from each holder, pick up and knit 2 new sts at base of ring finger = 12 (14) sts total. Work around in St st for approx. 2¼ (2½) in / 5.5 (6.5) cm. Shape fingertip with k2tog around until 8 sts rem. Cut yarn and draw end through rem sts; tighten.

Thumb: Place the held thumb sts onto a dpn; pick up and knit 3 sts across top of thumbhole = 16 (18) sts. Divide sts onto 3 dpn and work around in St st for approx. 2¼ (2½) in / 5.5 (6) cm. K2tog around until 8 sts rem. Cut yarn and draw end through rem sts; tighten.

Right-Hand Glove
Work as for left hand, reversing placement of thumb and fingers. Increase for thumb gusset on each side of the 2nd st of the rnd.

Weave in all ends neatly on WS.

TAM

SKILL LEVEL: Experienced
SIZES: Women's head circumference 22½-22¾ in /
57-58 cm
MATERIALS
Yarn:
CYCA #1 (fingering) Sølje from Hillesvåg (100%
Norwegian wool, 383 yd/350 m / 100 g)
Yarn Color and Amount:
Cognac 642103: 100 g
Needles:
U.S. size 2.5 / 3 mm: set of 5 dpn
GAUGE
25 sts in St st = 4 in / 10 cm.
Adjust needle size to obtain correct gauge if
necessary.

Tier 1: CO 6 sts. Work 12 rows back and forth in St
st = 1st block. Working through both loops, pick up
and knit 6 sts at right side of this block. Work 12 rows
in St st back and forth over the 6 sts = 2nd block.
Continue the same way, beginning each new block
on the right side of the previous block until you have
a total of 10 blocks.

Now begin working entrelac in the round.

Tier 2: Work whole blocks from right to left,
increasing to 8 sts on each block (increase both the
number of sts and rows—see Increases on page 14).
Tier 3: Work whole blocks from left to right,
increasing to 10 sts/rows per block.
Tier 4: Work whole blocks from right to left,
increasing to 12 sts/rows per block.
Tier 5: Work whole blocks from left to right,
increasing to 14 sts/rows per block.
Tier 6: Work whole blocks from right to left,
increasing to 16 sts/rows per block.
Tier 7: Work whole blocks from left to right,
decreasing to 14 sts/rows per block.

There should now be 140 sts around. Knit 1 rnd,
decreasing evenly spaced around to 130 sts. Work
8 rnds in k1, p1 ribbing. BO loosely. Use mattress
st to join the first block to the last one at the top of
the tam. Sew in a strand of yarn through the top of
the tam and tighten to close the center. Weave in all
ends neatly on WS.

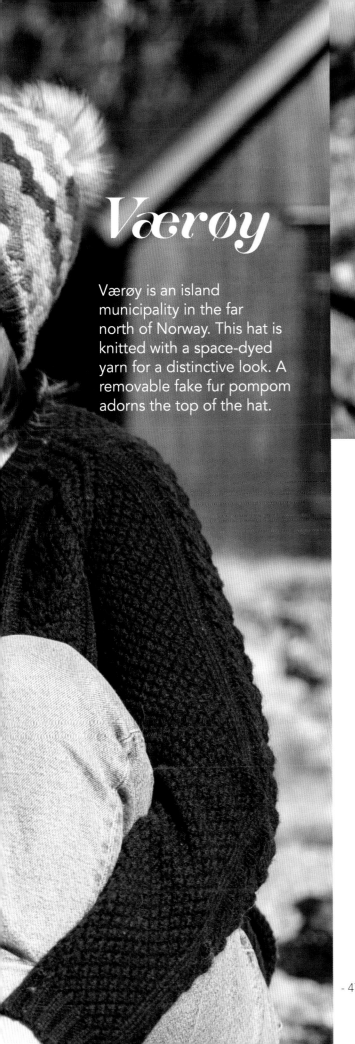

Værøy

Værøy is an island municipality in the far north of Norway. This hat is knitted with a space-dyed yarn for a distinctive look. A removable fake fur pompom adorns the top of the hat.

SKILL LEVEL: Experienced
SIZE: Women's
MATERIALS
Yarn:
  CYCA #1 (fingering) Nordlys from Viking Yarn
  (75% wool, 25% nylon, 383 yd/350 m / 100 g)
Yarn Color and Amount:
  Color 967: 100 g
Other Materials:
  1 fake fur pompom
Needles:
  U.S. size 2.5 / 3 mm: short circular
GAUGE
28 sts in St st = 4 in / 10 cm.
Adjust needle size to obtain correct gauge if necessary.

CO 120 sts. Join, being careful not to twist cast-on row. Work 10 rnds k2, p2 ribbing. Now begin entrelac in the round. Work 1 tier of 24 horizontal half blocks leaning from right to left, with 5 sts in each block. Work 16 tiers of whole blocks, changing block direction on each tier. End with the "star" shaping (see page 15).

Cut yarn and weave in all ends neatly on WS. Sew on a fake fur pompom or attach it with a snap for easy removal when washing hat.

Sock Knitting

Traditionally, entrelac has been most used for knitting socks. Looking at historic sources, we find that entrelac knitted stockings were "fancy" wear and often worn at weddings by both the bride and groom.

When Mette first discovered entrelac, it was while she was looking at sock patterns. We designed our own variations of entrelac socks with blocks both only on the leg and on the entire sock. With so many wonderful sock yarns now available, entrelac socks can be quite festive, whether you knit with colorful space-dyed yarns or single-color yarns.

Saga

ADULT-SIZE SOCKS
These socks have entrelac blocks on the legs.

SKILL LEVEL: Experienced
SIZES
Shoe Sizes: U. S. Women's 4½-6½ (7-9½, 10-12, Men's 10½-13) / Euro 35-37 (38-40, 41-43, 44-46)
Foot Length: 8½-9¼ (9¼-10, 10-10¾, 10¾-11¾) in / 21.3-23.2 (23.3-25.3, 25.3-27.3, 27.3-29.9) cm
MATERIALS
Yarn:
  CYCA #1 (fingering) Drops Fabel from Garnstudio (75% wool, 25% nylon, 224 yd/205 m / 50 g), 100 g
Yarn Colors and Amounts:
  Guacamole 151: 100 (100, 150, 150) g

Alternate 1: Sundown 310
Alternate 2: Burgundy 672
Alternate 3: Salt and Pepper 905
Alternate 4: Seafoam 910
Needles:
  U.S. size 1.5 / 2.5 mm: set of 5 dpn

GAUGE
24 sts in St st = 4 in / 10 cm.
Adjust needle size to obtain correct gauge if necessary.

———————————

CO 64 (72, 80, 80) sts. Divide sts evenly onto 4 dpn and join. Knit 1 rnd. Work 10 rnds in k2, p2 ribbing. Knit 1 rnd, decreasing by working k2tog with each pair of knit sts = 48 (54, 60, 60) sts rem. Now work entrelac in the round. Begin with 1 tier of 6 horizontal half blocks leaning from right to left, with 8 (9, 10, 10) sts in each block.

Continue with 7 (7, 8, 8) tiers of whole blocks, changing direction of blocks every tier.
Now knit 1 rnd, increasing evenly spaced around to the original number of sts = 64 (72, 80, 80) sts. Make sure there are an equal number of sts on each dpn. Now work 10 rnds of k2, p2 ribbing.

Heel Flap: The heel flap is worked over the 32 (36, 40, 40) sts on Ndls 1 and 4. Work back and forth in St st for 24 (28, 32, 32) rows.

Heel Turn: Begin at the center of the heel flap. K3, sl 1, k1, psso; turn.
Row 1: Sl 1 purlwise, p6, p2tog; turn.
Row 2: Sl 1, k6, sl 1, k1, psso; turn.
Rep Rows 1-2 until all the sts have been worked across and you are at an edge. If you prefer, work the heel turn with RS always facing to avoid turning and purling.

Foot: Knit the 4 sts on Ndl 1, pick up and knit 12 (14, 16, 16) sts along edge of heel flap. Knit across Ndls

2-3. Pick up and knit 12 (14, 16, 16) sts along edge of heel flap and knit the 4 sts on Ndl 4 = 64 (72, 80, 80) sts. Place the new sts onto Ndls 1 and 4 so there are 16 (18, 20, 20) sts on each needle. The rnd begins at center of sole. Work around in St st until foot, from back of heel, measures approx. 7 (7½, 8¼, 9) in / 18 (19, 21, 23) cm or to desired length before toe shaping.

Toe Shaping: Begin the round at center of sole. Work as follows:
Ndl 1: K13 (15, 17, 17), k2tog, k1.
Ndl 2: K1, sl 1, k1, psso, k13 (15, 17, 17).
Ndl 3: Work as for Ndl 1.
Ndl 4: Work as for Ndl 2.
There will be 1 st fewer on each needle every rnd. When 8 sts total rem, cut yarn. Draw end through rem sts and tighten.

Make the second sock the same way. Weave in all ends neatly on WS.

Saga

CHILDREN'S SOCKS

These children's socks have entrelac blocks on the legs.

SKILL LEVEL: Experienced

SIZES

Shoe Sizes: U. S. Toddler/Child's 6-7 (7-8, 9½-10, 11-11½ , 12-1, 1½-3) / Euro 22-23 (24-25, 26-27, 28-29, 30-32, 33-34)

Foot Length: 5-5½ (5½-6, 6-6½, 6½-7, 7-8, 8-8½) in / 12.7-14.1 (14.1-15.3, 15.3-16.6, 16.6-18, 18-20, 20-21.3) cm

MATERIALS

Yarn:

CYCA #1 (fingering) Drops Fabel from Garnstudio (75% wool, 25% nylon, 224 yd/205 m / 50 g)

Yarn Color and Amounts:

Tex-Mex 153: 100 (100, 100, 100, 100, 100) g

Needles:

U.S. size 1.5 / 2.5 mm: set of 5 dpn

GAUGE

24 sts in St st = 4 in / 10 cm.

Adjust needle size to obtain correct gauge if necessary.

CO 40 (43, 43, 48, 48, 56) sts. Divide sts evenly onto 4 dpn and join.

Sizes 6-7 (7-8, 9½-10) / Euro 22-23 (24-25, 26-27): Knit 8 rnds in St st. Knit 1 rnd, decreasing evenly spaced around to 30 (35, 35) sts.

Sizes 11-11½ (12-1, 1½-3) / Euro 28/29 (30/32, 33/34): Knit 1 rnd. Work 8 rnds in k2, p2 ribbing and then knit 1 rnd, decreasing by working k2tog with each pair of knit sts = 36 (36, 42) sts rem.

All sizes: Now work entrelac in the round. Begin with 1 tier of 6 (5, 5, 6, 6, 6) horizontal half blocks leaning from right to left, with 5 (7, 7, 6, 6, 7) sts in each block.

Continue with 3 (5, 6, 7, 7, 7) tiers of whole blocks, changing direction of blocks each tier. End with 1 tier of horizontal half blocks.

Now knit 1 rnd, increasing evenly spaced around to 40 (44, 44, 48, 48, 56) sts. Next, work 8 rnds of k2, p2 ribbing. Divide the sts onto 4 dpn with 10 (11, 11, 12, 12, 14) sts on each needle.

Heel Flap: The heel flap is worked over the 20 (22, 22, 24, 24, 28) sts on Ndls 1 and 4. Work back and forth in St st for 16 (18, 18, 20, 20, 24) rows.

Heel Turn: Begin at the center of the heel flap. K2, sl 1, k1, psso; turn.

Row 1: Sl 1 purlwise, p4, p2tog; turn.

Row 2: Sl 1, k4, sl 1, k1, psso; turn.

Rep Rows 1-2 until all the sts have been worked across and you are at an edge. If you prefer, work the heel turn with RS always facing to avoid turning and purling.

Foot: Knit the 3 sts on Ndl 1, pick up and knit 7 (8, 8, 9, 9, 11) sts along edge of heel flap. Knit across Ndls 2-3. Pick up and knit 7 (8, 8, 9, 9, 11) sts along edge of heel flap and knit the 3 sts on Ndl 4 = 40 (44, 44, 48, 48, 56) sts. Place the new sts onto Ndls 1 and 4 so there are the same number of sts on each needle. The rnd begins at center of sole. Work around in St st until foot, from back of heel, measures approx. 4½ (5¼, 5½, 6, 6¼, 6¾) in / 11.5 (13, 14, 15, 16, 17) cm or to desired length before toe shaping.

Toe Shaping: Begin the round at center of sole. Work as follows:

Ndl 1: K7 (8, 8, 9, 9, 11), k2tog, k1.

Ndl 2: K1, sl 1, k1, psso, k7 (8, 8, 9, 9, 11).

Ndl 3: Work as for Ndl 1.

Ndl 4: Work as for Ndl 2.

There will be 1 st fewer on each needle every rnd. When 8 sts total rem, cut yarn. Draw end through rem sts and tighten.

Make the second sock the same way. Weave in all ends neatly on WS.

Saga

BABY SOCKS
These baby socks have entrelac blocks on the legs.

SKILL LEVEL: Experienced
SIZES
Shoe Sizes: U. S. Baby 1-2 (2½-4, 4½-5½) / Euro 16-17 (18-19, 20-21)
Foot Length: 5-5½ (5½-6, 6-6½, 6½-7, 7-8, 8-8½) in / 8.3-9.9 (9.9-11.5, 11.5-12.7) cm
MATERIALS
Yarn:
CYCA #1 (fingering) Drops Fabel from Garnstudio (75% wool, 25% nylon, 224 yd/205 m / 50 g)
Yarn Colors and Amounts:
Guacamole 151: 50 (50, 50) g
Needles:
U.S. size 1.5 (1.5, 2.5) / 2.5 (2.5, 3) mm: set of 5 dpn
GAUGE
24 sts in St st = 4 in / 10 cm.
Adjust needle size to obtain correct gauge if necessary.

With dpn U.S. size 1.5 (1.5, 2.5) / 2.5 (2.5, 3) mm, CO 40 (40, 40) sts. Divide sts evenly onto 4 dpn and join. Knit 5 rnds in St st and then knit 1 rnd, decreasing 10 sts evenly spaced around = 30 (30, 30) sts rem.

Now work entrelac in the round. Begin with 1 tier of 6 horizontal half blocks leaning from right to left, with 5 (5, 5) sts in each block.

Continue with 3 (3, 3) tiers (or to desired length) of whole blocks, changing direction of blocks each tier. End with 1 tier of horizontal half blocks.

Now, knit 1 rnd, increasing evenly spaced around to the original stitch count = 40 (40, 40) sts. Next, work 6 rnds of k2, p2 ribbing.

Heel Flap: The heel flap is worked over the 20 (20, 20) sts on Ndls 1 and 4. Work back and forth in St st for 14 (14, 14) rows.

Heel Turn: Begin at the center of the heel flap. K2, sl 1, k1, psso; turn.
Row 1: Sl 1 purlwise, p4, p2tog; turn.
Row 2: Sl 1, k4, sl 1, k1, psso; turn.
Rep Rows 1-2 until all the sts have been worked across and you are at an edge. If you prefer, work the heel turn with RS always facing to avoid turning and purling.

Foot: Knit the 3 sts on Ndl 1, pick up and knit 7 (7, 7) sts along edge of heel flap. Knit across Ndls 2-3. Pick up and knit 7 (7, 7) sts along edge of heel flap and knit the 3 sts on Ndl 4 = 40 (40, 40) sts. Place the new sts onto Ndls 1 and 4 so there are the same number of sts on each needle. The rnd begins at center of sole. Work around in St st until foot, from back of heel, measures approx. 3¼ (3¾, 4¼) in / 8 (9.5, 11) cm or to desired length before toe shaping.

Toe Shaping: Begin the round at center of sole. Work as follows:
Ndl 1: K7 (7, 7), k2tog, k1.
Ndl 2: K1, sl 1, k1, psso, k7 (7, 7).
Ndl 3: Work as for Ndl 1.
Ndl 4: Work as for Ndl 2.
There will be 1 st fewer on each needle every rnd. When 8 sts total rem, cut yarn. Draw end through rem sts and tighten.

Make the second sock the same way. Weave in all ends neatly on WS.

Crowberry

These socks are knitted all over in entrelac,
which results in very elastic socks that will
fit well. For this pattern, we used a colorful
yarn in fingering weight.

ADULT-SIZE SOCKS

SKILL LEVEL: Experienced
SIZES
Shoe Sizes: U. S. Women's 4-6½ (7½-9½,
   Men's 10-12) / Euro 35-37 (38-40, 41-43)
Foot Length: 8½-9¼ (9¼-10, 10-10¾) in / 21.3-23.2
   (23.2-25.3, 25.3-27.3) cm
MATERIALS
Yarn:
   CYCA #1 (fingering) Magi from Rauma (75% wool,
   25% nylon, 230 yd/210 m / 50 g)
Yarn Amounts:
   100 (150, 150) g
Needles:
   U.S. size 1.5 / 2.5 mm: set of 5 dpn
GAUGE
27 sts in St st = 4 in / 10 cm.
Adjust needle size to obtain correct gauge if
necessary.

CO 56 (64, 72) sts. Divide sts evenly onto 4 dpn and
join. Knit 1 rnd. Work 8 rnds in k2, p2 ribbing. Knit
1 rnd, decreasing by working k2tog with each pair
of knit sts = 42 (48, 54) sts rem. Now work entrelac
in the round. Begin with 1 tier of 6 horizontal half

blocks leaning from right to left, with 7 (8, 9) sts in
each block. Continue with 6 (7, 7) tiers of whole
blocks, alternately tiers leaning left and right.

Heel: See schematic below. The heel is worked over
half of the sts.
Blocks 1-3: Work 3 whole blocks leaning to the left.
Pick up and knit at top of Block 3.
Blocks 4-5: Work 2 whole blocks leaning to the right.
Pick up and knit at top of Block 5.
Block 6: Work 1 block leaning to the left.
Block 7: Pick up and knit sts in Block 4 and join
them to Block 6.
Block 8: Pick up and knit sts in Block 6 and join
them to Block 5.
Block 9: Pick up and knit sts in Block 1 and join
them to Block 8.
Block 10: Pick up and knit sts in Block 8 and join
them to Block 7.
Block 11: Pick up and knit sts in Block 7 and join
them to Block 3.

Now work all around in entrelac until there are 7
(8, 8) new tiers of whole blocks. Finish with a "star"
shaping (see page 15).

Make the second sock the same way. Weave in all
ends neatly on WS.

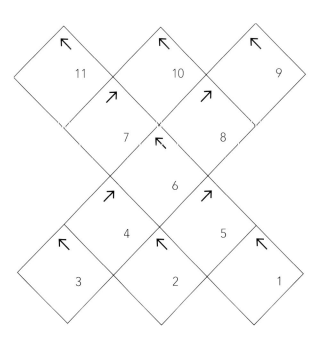

Crowberry

CHILDREN'S SOCKS

These children's socks are knitted all over in entrelac, which results in very elastic socks that will fit well. We used a fingering weight yarn, and crowned these socks with Latvian braids.

SKILL LEVEL: Experienced

SIZES

Shoe Sizes: U. S. Toddler/Child's 4½-6½ (11-11½, 1½-3) / Euro 20-22 (28-29, 33-34)

Foot Length: 4½-5 (6½-7, 8-8½) in / 11.5-12.7 (16.6-18, 20-21.3) cm

MATERIALS

Yarn:
CYCA #1 (fingering) Drops Fabel from Garnstudio (75% wool, 25% nylon, 224 yd/205 m / 50 g)

Yarn Colors and Amounts:
Color 1: Natural 100: 50 (50, 50) g
Color 2: Cerise 109: 50 (50, 50) g

Needles:
U.S. size 1.5 / 2.5 mm: set of 5 dpn

GAUGE

27 sts in St st = 4 in / 10 cm.
Adjust needle size to obtain correct gauge if necessary.

With Cerise and dpn, CO 40 (48, 56) sts. Divide sts evenly over 4 dpn and join. Work a two-end purl braid (see page 16). Next, knit 1 rnd with Cerise, decreasing evenly spaced around to 30 (36, 42) sts.

Now work around in entrelac: Work 1 tier of 6 horizontal half blocks, leaning from right to left, with 5 (6, 7) sts in each Cerise block. Next, work 5 (7, 7) tiers of whole blocks, changing direction of blocks on each tier and alternating Natural and Cerise tiers. The first whole block tier is worked with Natural.

Heel: See schematic below. The heel is worked over half the stitches. All the blocks are worked in Cerise.
Blocks 1-3: Work 3 whole blocks leaning to the left. Pick up and knit at top of Block 3.
Blocks 4-5: Work 2 whole Blocks leaning to the right. Pick up and knit at top of Block 5.
Block 6: Work 1 block leaning to the left.
Block 7: Pick up and knit sts in Block 4 and join them to Block 6.
Block 8: Pick up and knit sts in Block 6 and join them to Block 5.
Block 9: Pick up and knit sts in Block 1 and join them to Block 8.
Block 10: Pick up and knit sts in Block 8 and join them to Block 7.
Block 11: Pick up and knit sts in Block 7 and join them to Block 3.

Now work all around in entrelac (alternating tiers of Cerise and Natural) until there are 7 (7, 8) new tiers of whole blocks. Finish with a "star" shaping (see page 15).

Make the second sock the same way.
Weave in all ends neatly on WS.

Knits for Children

After having designed so many accessories, we felt the need for some new challenges. Every child deserves good knitwear—so why not make some children's clothes with entrelac? We've created several patterns, both for small children and for children a bit older. Entrelac offers many options for playing with colors, which is great for really fun children's outfits. If you choose a yarn with good texture and luster, a single-color garment will look subtle but pretty. In other words, you can express your individual taste.

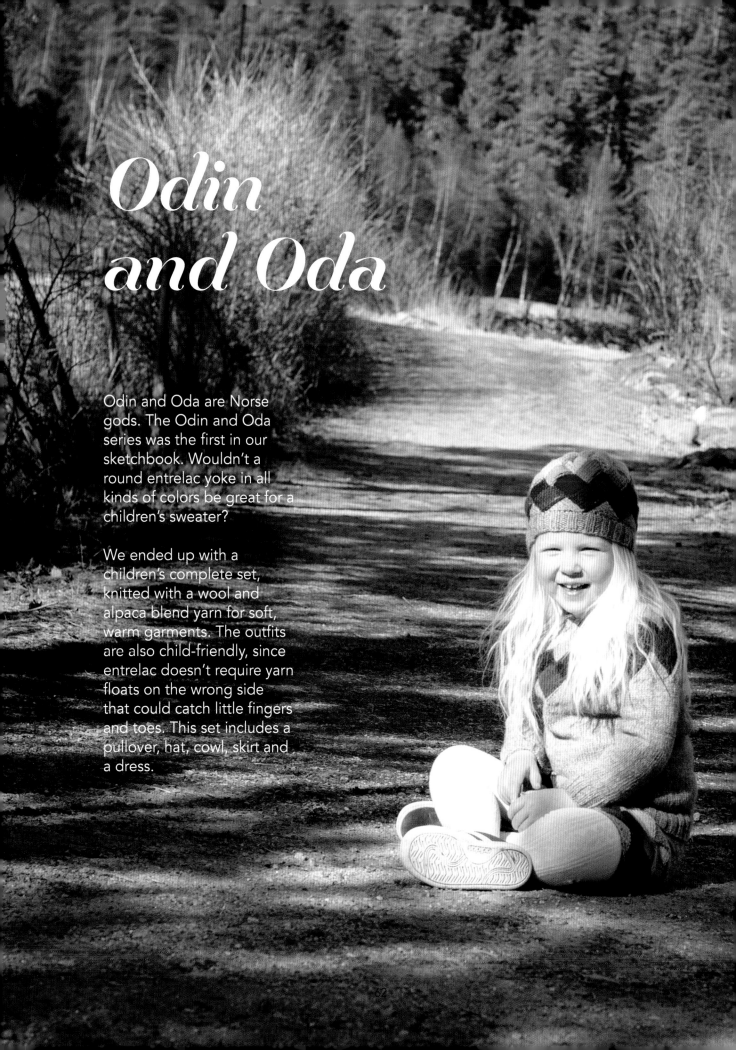

Odin and Oda

Odin and Oda are Norse gods. The Odin and Oda series was the first in our sketchbook. Wouldn't a round entrelac yoke in all kinds of colors be great for a children's sweater?

We ended up with a children's complete set, knitted with a wool and alpaca blend yarn for soft, warm garments. The outfits are also child-friendly, since entrelac doesn't require yarn floats on the wrong side that could catch little fingers and toes. This set includes a pullover, hat, cowl, skirt and a dress.

SET WITH PULLOVER, HAT, SKIRT, DRESS, AND COWL

COLOR COMBINATIONS FOR THE PULLOVER, HAT, COWL, AND SKIRT

GRAY/YELLOW VERSION:
COLOR 1: Gray SFN41
COLOR 2: White SFN10
COLOR 3: Beige SFN61
COLOR 4: Ochre 7255
COLOR 5: Dark Gray SFN43
COLOR 6: Charcoal Gray SFN75

LIGHT BLUE/PINK VERSION:
COLOR 1: Light Blue/Gray 7244
COLOR 2: White SFN10
COLOR 3: Light Pink 8401
COLOR 4: Purple 8126
COLOR 5: Light Purple 0022
COLOR 6: Salmon Pink 1832

GRAY/RED-BROWN VERSION:
COLOR 1: Light Gray SFN41
COLOR 2: Light Olive 8287
COLOR 3: Olive 2196
COLOR 4: Red 6085
COLOR 5: Rust Red 2230
COLOR 6: Burgundy 3083

PULLOVER

This pullover is knitted from the top down. It begins with a ribbed neckband and then shifts to an entrelac yoke. After that, you can decide whether to knit the body or the sleeves next. To shape the yoke, stitches are added to the blocks from tier to tier. It's also easy to adjust the length of body and sleeves when you work from the top down.

SKILL LEVEL: Experienced
SIZES: 3-4 (5-6, 7-8, 9-10) years
FINISHED MEASUREMENTS
Chest: 24½ (26, 27¼, 28¾) in / 62 (66, 69, 73) cm
Total Length: 15 (17, 18¼, 19¾) in / 38 (43, 46, 50) cm
Sleeve Length: 10¾ (12¼, 14½, 16½) in / 27 (31, 37, 42) cm
MATERIALS
Yarn:
 CYCA #3 (DK, light worsted) Mitu from Rauma (50% wool, 50% alpaca, 109 yd/100 m / 50 g)
Yarn Colors and Amounts:
 Color 1: 250 (300, 350, 350) g
 Color 2: 50 (50, 50, 50) g
 Color 3: 50 (50, 50, 50) g
 Color 4: 50 (50, 50, 50) g
 Color 5: 50 (50, 50, 50) g
 Color 6: 0 (50, 50, 50) g
Needles:
 U. S. sizes 4 and 6 / 3.5 and 4 mm: set of 5 dpn and 16 and 24 in / 40 and 60 cm circulars
GAUGE
22 sts in St st on larger needles = 4 in / 10 cm. Adjust needle size to obtain correct gauge if necessary.

Yoke

With smaller circular and Color 1, CO 84 (88, 96, 104) sts. Join, being careful not to twist cast-on row; pm for beginning of rnd. Work around in k2, p2 ribbing for 1¼ (1¼, 1½, 1½) in / 3 (3, 4, 4) cm. Change to larger circular. Knit 1 rnd, decreasing 14 (28, 21, 14) sts evenly spaced around = 70 (60, 75, 90) sts.

Now work entrelac in the round. Begin the round at center back so the blocks will be symmetrically arranged around the yoke.
Tier 1: Continue with Color 1 and work the tier with 14 (15, 15, 15) horizontal half blocks, leaning from right to left, with 5 (4, 5, 6) sts in each block.

Tier 2: Change to Color 2. Work the tier with whole blocks, leaning from left to right, with 6 (5, 5, 6) sts in each block.
Tier 3: Change to Color 3. Work the tier with whole blocks, leaning from right to left, with 7 (6, 7, 7) sts in each block.
Tier 4: Change to Color 4. Work the tier with whole blocks, leaning from left to right, with 8 (8, 9, 10) sts in each block.
Tier 5: Change to Color 5. Work the tier with whole blocks, leaning from right to left, with 10 (9, 10, 11) sts in each block.

Size 3-4 years:
Tier 6: Change to Color 1. Work 1 tier of horizontal half blocks leaning from left to right with 10 sts in each block. The entrelac section of the yoke is now finished. Skip to "All sizes" below.

Sizes (5-6, 7-8, 9-10) years:
Tier 6: Change to Color 6. Work 1 tier with whole blocks leaning from left to right, with (11, 12, 13) sts in each block.
Tier 7: Change to Color 1. Work 1 tier of horizontal half blocks leaning from right to left, with (11, 12, 13) sts in each block.

All Sizes:
There should now be 140 (164, 180, 195) sts around. Continue in Color 1 and St st. On the first rnd after the tier of half blocks, M1 between each st. On the next rnd, decrease evenly spaced around to 212 (228, 240, 258) sts. These two rounds help avoid any holes between the entrelac and St st—a little extra work, but well worth it!

On the next rnd, divide the sts for the body and sleeves: K31 (33, 35, 37), place the next 44 (48, 50, 55) sts on a holder for a sleeve, CO 6 new sts for underarm, k62 (66, 70, 74), place the next 44 (48, 50, 55) sts on a holder for a sleeve, CO 6 new sts for underarm, k31 (33, 35, 37).

Body
The body has 136 (144, 152, 160) sts. Continue around in St st with Color 1 until body measures 9 (9½, 9¾, 10¾) in / 23 (24, 25, 27) cm from rnd between entrelac yoke and body. Change to smaller circular. Knit 1 rnd, and, *at the same time*, increase 12 sts evenly spaced around = 148 (156, 164, 172) sts. Work around in k2, p2 ribbing for 1¼ (1¼, 1½, 1½) in / 3 (3, 4, 4) cm. BO in ribbing.

Sleeves

Divide the held sts of one sleeve onto 4 larger dpn, CO 6 sts at underarm (pm at center of the underarm) = 50 (54, 56, 61) sts. With Color 1, work around in St st. When sleeve measures ¾ in / 2 cm from rnd separating entrelac and St st, decrease 1 st on each side of marker. Decrease the same way approx. every 1½ in / 4 cm a total of 5 (6, 6, 8) times = 40 (42, 44, 45) sts rem. When sleeve measures 9½ (11, 13, 15) in / 24 (28, 33, 38) cm, change to smaller dpn and work around in k2, p2 ribbing for 1¼ (1¼, 1½, 1½) in / 3 (3, 4, 4) cm. BO in ribbing. Make the second sleeve the same way.

Finishing

Seam the underarms. Weave in all ends neatly on WS.

HAT

Here's an easy hat to go with the children's Odin and Oda pullover. This hat suits both boys and girls.

SKILL LEVEL: Experienced
SIZES: 2-5 (7-10) years
FINISHED MEASUREMENTS
Circumference: 15¾ (17¼) in / 40 (44) cm. You can adjust the sizing somewhat by changing gauge/ needle size.
MATERIALS
Yarn:
   CYCA #3 (DK, light worsted) Mitu from Rauma (50% wool, 50% alpaca, 109 yd/100 m / 50 g)
Yarn Colors and Amounts:
   Color 1: 50 (50) g
   Color 2: 50 (50) g
   Color 3: 50 (50) g
   Color 4: 50 (50) g
   Color 5: 50 (50) g
   Color 6: 50 (50) g
Needles:
   U. S. sizes 2.5 and 6 / 3 and 4 mm: 16 in / 40 cm circular
GAUGE
22 sts in St st on larger needles = 4 in / 10 cm.
Adjust needle size to obtain correct gauge if necessary.

With smaller needles and Color 1, CO 84 (90) sts. Join, being careful not to twist cast-on row; pm for beginning of rnd. Work 8 rnds in k2, p2 ribbing. Knit 1 rnd, decreasing evenly spaced to 72 (80) sts.

Now change to larger circular and begin working entrelac in the round.

Tier 1, with Color 1: Work 9 (10) horizontal half blocks leaning from right to left, with 8 sts in each block.
Tier 2, with Color 6: Work whole blocks leaning from left to right.
Tier 3, with Color 5: Work whole blocks leaning from right to left.
Tier 4, with Color 4: Work whole blocks leaning from left to right.
Tier 5, with Color 3: Work whole blocks leaning from right to left.
Tier 6, with Color 2: Finish with a "star" shaping (see page 15).
Cut yarn and weave in all ends neatly on WS.

For sizes 2-5 years:
Finish with Color 1 and a "star" shaping (see page 15) on Tier 5. Fasten off yarns.

SKIRT

The skirt is worked from the bottom up with entrelac around the bottom edge and then stockinette up to the waist. A casing at the waist for an elastic band ensures the skirt will fit well.

SKILL LEVEL: Experienced
SIZES: 3-4 (5-6, 7-8, 9-10) years
FINISHED MEASUREMENTS
Circumference at Waist: 19 (20½, 22, 23¾) in / 48 (52, 56, 60) cm
Total Length: 9½ (11, 12¾, 14¼) in / 24 (28, 32, 36) cm
MATERIALS
Yarn:
  CYCA #3 (DK, light worsted) Mitu from Rauma (50% wool, 50% alpaca, 109 yd/100 m / 50 g)
Yarn Colors and Amounts:
  Color 1: 100 (100, 150, 150) g
  Color 2: 50 (50, 50, 50) g
  Color 3: 50 (50, 50, 50) g
  Color 4: 50 (50, 50, 50) g
  Color 5: 50 (50, 50, 50) g
  Color 6: 0 (50, 50, 50) g
Other Materials:
  Waistband elastic, long enough to go around waist + seam allowance
Needles:
  U. S. size 6 / 4 mm: short circular
GAUGE
22 sts in St st on larger needles = 4 in / 10 cm. Adjust needle size to obtain correct gauge if necessary.

———————————————

With Color 1 and the elastic cast-on technique (see page 10), CO 112 (120, 126, 135) sts. Join, being careful not to twist cast-on row; pm for beginning of rnd.
Begin working entrelac in the round.

Tier 1, with Color 1: Work 14 (15, 14, 15) horizontal half blocks leaning from right to left, with 8 (8, 9, 9) sts in each block.
Tier 2, with Color 2: Work whole blocks leaning from left to right.

Tier 3, with Color 3: Work whole blocks leaning from right to left.
Tier 4, with Color 4: Work whole blocks leaning from left to right.

Size 3-4 years:
Tier 5, with Color 1: Work horizontal half blocks leaning from right to left. The entrelac section is now complete—skip to the section for All Sizes.

Sizes (5-6, 7-8, 9-10) years:
Tier 5, with Color 5: Work whole blocks leaning from right to left.
Tier 6, with Color 1: Work horizontal half blocks leaning from left to right.

All Sizes:
The rnd now begins at center back of the skirt. On the next rnd, work in St st and, *at the same time*, increase evenly spaced around to 152 (160, 168, 176) sts and pm as follows: after 19 (20, 21, 22) sts; after 38 (40, 42, 44) sts; after 38 (40, 42, 44) sts; after 38 (40, 42, 44) sts; 19 (20, 21, 22) sts rem to end of rnd. Knit around in St st for ¾ (1, 1¼, 1½) in / 2 (2.5, 3, 3.5) cm.

On the next rnd, continue in St st and decrease as follows: k2tog on left side of each marker and k2tog tbl on right side of each marker. Decrease the same way every ¾ (1, 1¼, 1½) in / 2 (2.5, 3, 3.5) cm a total of 6 times = 104 (112, 120, 128) sts rem. Continue in St st without further shaping until skirt measures 9½ (11, 12¾, 14¼) in / 24 (28, 32, 36) cm. Purl 1 rnd for foldline. Knit 3 rnds. On the next rnd, BO the first 4 sts of the rnd and then knit to end of rnd. On the following rnd, CO 4 sts over the 4 bound-off sts of previous rnd. Knit 3 rnds over all sts. BO loosely.

Finishing
Fold casing and sew down on WS. Thread elastic band through casing and seam ends. Weave in all ends neatly on WS.

DRESS

This dress is worked from the top down, with an entrelac yoke. Garter stitch forms the edging for the neck and lower hem.

SKILL LEVEL: Experienced
SIZES: 3-4 (5-6, 7-8) years
FINISHED MEASUREMENTS
Chest: 24 (25½, 27¼) in / 61 (65, 69) cm
Total Length: 24 (26¾, 29½) in / 61 (68, 75) cm
MATERIALS
Yarn:
   CYCA #3 (DK, light worsted) Mitu from Rauma (50% wool, 50% alpaca, 109 yd/100 m / 50 g)
Yarn Colors and Amounts:
   Color 1: Salmon Pink 1832: 200 (250, 300) g
   Color 2: White SFN10: 50 (50, 50) g
   Color 3: Light Pink 8401: 50 (50, 50) g
   Color 4: Light Blue 7244: 50 (50, 50) g
   Color 5: Grey-Blue 0512: 50 (50, 50) g
   Color 6: Denim Blue 4967: 50 (50, 50) g
Needles:
   U. S. sizes 2.5 and 6 / 3 and 4 mm: set of 5 dpn and circular; U. S. size 4 / 3.5 mm: circular
Crochet Hook:
   U. S. size G-8 / 4 mm: optional for underarm finishing
GAUGE
22 sts in St st on larger needles = 4 in / 10 cm. Adjust needle size to obtain correct gauge if necessary.

Yoke

With Color 1 and short circular U. S. size 6 / 4 mm, CO 84 (88, 96) sts. Join, being careful not to twist cast-on row; pm for beginning of rnd. Work garter st in the rnd (alternate knit 1 rnd, purl 1 rnd) for ¾ in / 2 cm. Change to short circular U. S. size 4 / 3.5 mm. Knit 1 rnd decreasing evenly spaced around to 70 (60, 75) sts.

Now begin entrelac in the round.

Tier 1, with Color 1: Work 14 (15, 15) horizontal half blocks leaning from right to left, with 5 (4, 5) sts in each block.
Tier 2, with Color 2: Work whole blocks leaning from left to right with 6 (5, 6) sts in each block.
Tier 3, with Color 3: Work whole blocks leaning from right to left with 7 (6, 7) sts in each block.
Tier 4, with Color 4: Work whole blocks leaning from left to right with 9 (8, 9) sts in each block

Tier 5, with Color 5: Work whole blocks leaning from right to left with 11 (10, 11) sts in each block.

Size 3-4 years:
Tier 6, with Color 1: Work with horizontal half blocks leaning from left to right with 11 sts in each block. The entrelac section is now complete—skip to All Sizes.

Sizes (5-6, 7-8) years:
Tier 6, with Color 6: Work whole blocks leaning from left to right with (12, 13) sts in each block.
Tier 7, with Color 1: Work with horizontal half blocks leaning from right to left with (12, 13) sts in each block.

All Sizes:
There should now be 154 (180, 195) sts around. Continuing in St st with Color 1, on the next rnd, M1 between each st. On the following rnd, decease evenly spaced around to 212 (228, 244) sts. These two rounds help avoid any holes between the entrelac and St st—a little extra work, but well worth it!

Change to U. S. 6 / 4 mm circular. Divide for body and sleeves as follows: K31 (33, 35), loosely BO next 44 (48, 52) sts for sleeve, k62 (66, 70) sts, loosely BO next 44 (48, 52) sts for sleeve, k31 (33, 35). On the next rnd, CO 6 sts at each underarm = 136 (144, 152) sts.

On the next rnd, place 4 stitch markers: K17 (18, 19), pm, [k34 (36, 38), pm] 3 times, k17 (18, 19). Knit around in St st for 1½ (1½, 2) in / 4 (4, 5) cm. Now increase 1 st on each side of each marker, every 3¼ (3½, 4) in / 8 (9, 10) cm, a total of 6 times = 184 (192, 200) sts. Work 1½ in / 4 cm in garter st (= alternately knit 1 rnd, purl 1 rnd). BO loosely.

Finishing
Weave in all ends neatly on WS. If desired, for a smooth and neat finish for underarms slip st crochet across the 6 cast-on sts at each underarm.

COWL

A cowl is an easy way to keep a child warm when they won't hold still long enough to put on a sweater! This cowl is worked from the top down, with entrelac encircling the shoulders and chest.

SKILL LEVEL: Experienced
SIZES: 3-4 (5-6, 7-8, 9-10) years
MATERIALS
Yarn:
   CYCA #3 (DK, light worsted), Mitu from Rauma (50% wool, 50% alpaca, 109 yd/100 m / 50 g)
Yarn Colors and Amounts:
   Color 1: 50 (50, 50, 50) g
   Color 2: 50 (50, 50, 50) g
   Color 3: 50 (50, 50, 50) g
   Color 4: 50 (50, 50, 50) g
   Color 5: 50 (50, 50, 50) g
   Color 6: 0 (50, 50, 50) g
Needles:
   U. S. sizes 4 and 6 / 3.5 and 4 mm: short circulars
GAUGE
22 sts in St st on larger needles = 4 in / 10 cm. Adjust needle size to obtain correct gauge if necessary.

YOKE

With Color 1 and smaller circular, CO 84 (88, 96, 104) sts. Join, being careful not to twist cast-on row; pm for beginning of rnd. Work in k2, p2 ribbing for 3¼ (3¼, 3½, 3½) in / 8 (8, 9, 9) cm. Change to larger circular. Knit 1 rnd, decreasing 14 (28, 21, 14) sts evenly spaced around to 70 (60, 75, 90) sts.

Now begin entrelac in the round.
Tier 1, with Color 1: Work 14 (15, 15, 15) horizontal half blocks leaning from right to left, with 5 (4, 5, 6) sts in each block.
Tier 2, with Color 2: Work whole blocks leaning from left to right with 6 (5, 5, 6) sts in each block.
Tier 3, with Color 3: Work whole blocks leaning from right to left with 7 (6, 7, 7) sts in each block.
Tier 4, with Color 4: Work whole blocks leaning from left to right with 8 (8, 9, 10) sts in each block.
Tier 5, with Color 5: Work whole blocks leaning from right to left with 10 (9, 10, 11) sts in each block.

Size 3-4 years:
Tier 6, with Color 1: Work with horizontal half blocks leaning from left to right with 10 sts in each block. The entrelac section is now complete—skip to All Sizes.

Sizes (5-6, 7-8, 9-10) years:
Tier 6, with Color 6: Work whole blocks leaning from left to right with (11, 12, 13) sts in each block.
Tier 7, with Color 1: Work with horizontal half blocks leaning from right to left with (11, 12, 13) sts in each block.

Final Shaping All Sizes
BO loosely, but, *at the same time*, M1 after every 3rd st; BO new sts in sequence. This technique produces an elastic edge.

Silja

Silja is the name of a lake in Central Sweden. This skirt is easy to knit. It suits all ages and can go with many different outfits. The entrelac knitting makes the skirt very elastic and comfortable to wear. It is worked from the top down, so it's easy to adjust the length to suit the person wearing it.

CHILDREN'S SKIRT

SKILL LEVEL: Experienced
SIZES: 2-4 (6-8, 9-11, 12-14) years
FINISHED MEASUREMENTS
Circumference at Waist: 16¼ (17, 18½, 19¼) in / 41 (43, 47, 49) cm
Length: 10¼ (11½, 14¼, 15½) in / 26 (29, 36, 39) cm
MATERIALS
Yarn:
    CYCA #3 (DK, light worsted) Drops Cotton Merino from Garnstudio (50% cotton, 50% Merino wool, 120 yd/110 m / 50 g)
Yarn Colors and Amounts:
    100 (150, 200, 250) g
Color Suggestions:
    Choice 1: Coral 13
    Choice 2: Pistachio 10
    Choice 3: Denim Blue 16
Needles:
    U. S. sizes 2.5 and 6 / 3 and 4 mm: short circulars
GAUGE
22 sts in St st on larger needles = 4 in / 10 cm.
Adjust needle size to obtain correct gauge if necessary.

With smaller circular, CO 90 (94, 104, 108) sts. Join, being careful not to twist cast-on row; pm for beginning of rnd. Work around in k1, p1 ribbing for 2 in / 5 cm. Change to larger circular. Knit 1 rnd, *at the same time* decreasing evenly spaced around to 63 (70, 77, 84) sts.

Now begin entrelac knitting in the round.

Tier 1: Knit 1 tier with 9 (10, 11, 12) horizontal half blocks, leaning from right to left, with 7 sts in each block.
Tiers 2-3: Work 2 tiers of whole blocks.
Tier 4: Increase to 8 sts in each block.
Work 5 (6, 7, 8) tiers with 8 sts in each block.

On the next tier, increase to 9 sts in each block. Work 1 (1, 2, 2) tiers with 9 sts in each block.
Last tier: Work around in horizontal half blocks with 9 sts in each block = 81 (90, 99, 108) sts around.

Knit 1 rnd over all sts, increasing evenly spaced around to 102 (112, 124, 130) sts.

Change to smaller circular and end with 4 rnds k1, p1 ribbing. Loosely BO in ribbing. Weave in all ends neatly on WS.

Twins

This pullover is knitted around in stockinette from the bottom up, divided for front and back at the sleeves, and then worked back and forth in entrelac. Instead of traditional ribbed edges, entrelac graces the sleeve cuffs and lower edge of the body.

PULLOVER

SKILL LEVEL: Experienced
SIZES: 4 (6, 8, 10, 12, 14) years
FINISHED MEASUREMENTS
Chest: 24½ (25½, 27¼, 29½, 32¼, 34¼) in / 62 (65, 69, 75, 82, 87) cm
Total Length: 15 (16¼, 17¾, 19¼, 21¼, 23¾) in / 38 (41, 45, 49, 54, 60) cm
Sleeve Length: 12¼ (13, 13¾, 15½, 17, 17¾) in / 31 (33, 35, 39, 43, 45) cm
MATERIALS
Yarn:
   CYCA #3 (DK, light worsted) Tinde Pelsullgarn from Hillesvåg (100% Norwegian wool, 284 yd/260 m / 100 g)
Yarn Color and Amounts:
   200 (200, 300, 300, 400, 400) g
Color: Petrol 65210 OR Dungaree Blue 652113
Needles:
   U. S. sizes 4 and 6 / 3.5 and 4 mm: circulars and set of 5 dpn
GAUGE
22 sts in St st on larger needles = 4 in / 10 cm. Adjust needle size to obtain correct gauge if necessary.

––––––––––––––––––––––

Body
With smaller circular and elastic cast-on (see page 16), CO 90 (95, 100, 110, 120, 130) sts. Join, being careful not to twist sts; pm for beginning of rnd.

Work the entrelac lower edge: Knit 18 (19, 20, 22, 24, 26) horizontal half blocks leaning from right to left, with 5 sts in each block. Next, work 2 tiers of whole blocks and then 1 tier horizontal half blocks. Don't forget to change direction of blocks each tier.

Knit 1 rnd over all the sts, and, *at the same time*, increase evenly spaced around to 136 (144, 152, 164, 180, 192) sts. Change to larger circular and work around in St st until piece measures 10¾ (11½, 12¾, 14, 15½, 17½) in / 27 (29, 32.5, 35.5, 39.5, 44.5) cm.

Knit 1 rnd, decreasing evenly spaced around to 84 (96, 108, 120, 132, 144) sts. Divide body for back and front = 42 (48, 54, 60, 66, 72) sts for each piece.

Back
Now work back and forth in entrelac. Work 1 tier with 7 (8, 9, 10, 11, 12) horizontal half blocks leaning from right to left, with 6 sts in each block. Pick up and knit an extra st between the last st of the back and first st of front; work 1 vertical half block. The extra st is an edge st on the vertical block. Maintain the edge st as you continue. Work 1 tier of whole blocks from left to right. Pick up and knit an extra st between the last st of back and first st of front and work 1 vertical half block on this side also. The extra st is an edge st on the vertical block. Maintain the edge sts as you work up. Continue with whole blocks and vertical blocks at each side until there are a total of 6 (6, 7, 7, 8, 8) tiers of whole blocks. Finish with 1 tier of horizontal half blocks. Place the 24 (30, 30, 24, 36, 30) center sts on a holder for the neck.

Shoulders: BO loosely, but, *at the same time*, M1 after every 3rd st; BO new sts in sequence. This technique produces an elastic edge.

Front
Work as for back until there are a total of 5 (5, 6, 6, 7, 7) tiers, including the first horizontal half blocks. On the next tier, work as indicated on the schematic on the next page.
NOTE: Place the sts from the horizontal half blocks on a holder.

Tier 6 (6, 7, 7, 8, 8):
Size 4 years: Work 1 vertical half block, 2 whole blocks, 2 horizontal half blocks, 2 whole blocks, and 1 vertical half block.
Size 6 years: Work 1 vertical half block, 2 whole blocks, 3 horizontal half blocks, 2 whole blocks, and 1 vertical half block.
Size 8 years: Work 3 whole blocks, 3 horizontal half blocks, 3 whole blocks.
Size 10 years: Work 4 whole blocks, 2 horizontal half blocks, 4 whole blocks.
Size 12 years: Work 1 vertical half block, 3 whole blocks, 4 horizontal half blocks, 3 whole blocks, and 1 vertical half block.
Size 14 years: Work 1 vertical half block, 4 whole blocks, 3 horizontal half blocks, 4 whole blocks, and 1 vertical half block.

Now work each of the shoulders separately.

Left Shoulder
Tier 7 (7, 8, 8, 9, 9):
Size 4 years: Work 2 whole blocks.
Size 6 years: Work 2 whole blocks.
Size 8 years: Work 1 vertical half block and 2 whole blocks.
Size 10 years: Work 1 vertical half blocks and 3 whole blocks.
Size 12 years: Work 3 whole blocks.
Size 14 years: Work 4 whole blocks.

Tier 8 (8, 9, 9, 10, 10):
Size 4 years: Work 1 quarter block and 1 horizontal half block.
Size 6 years: Work 1 quarter block and 1 horizontal half block.
Size 8 years: Work 2 horizontal half blocks.
Size 10 years: Work 3 horizontal half blocks.
Size 12 years: Work 1 quarter block and 2 horizontal half blocks.
Size 14 years: Work 1 quarter block and 3 horizontal half blocks.
BO loosely as for back.

Right Shoulder
Work as for left shoulder but in reverse to match.

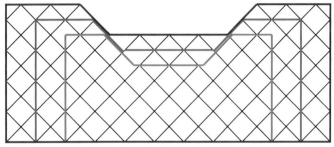

12 years   8 years   4 years

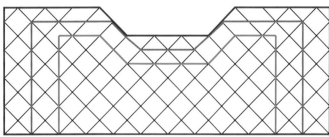

14 years   10 years   6 years

Sleeves
Wth smaller dpn, CO 25 (30, 30, 35, 35, 40) sts. Join and pm for beginning of rnd. Begin with the entrelac edge: Work 5 (6, 6, 7, 7, 8) horizontal half blocks leaning from right to left, with 5 sts per block. Next, work 2 tiers of whole blocks and then 1 tier of horizontal half blocks. Knit 1 rnd, *at the same time* increasing evenly spaced around to 30 (32, 36, 38, 40, 42) sts. Change to larger dpn and St st. On every 6th rnd, increase on after the first and before the last st until there are a total of 48 (52, 54, 60, 64, 68) sts. Continue in St st until sleeve is 12¼ (13, 13¾, 15½, 17, 17¾) in / 31 (33, 35, 39, 43, 45) cm long. BO loosely. Make the second sleeve the same way.

Finishing
Seam shoulders, sewing inside first stitch loops. Attach sleeves. We suggest that you *very gently* steam press the entrelac (under a damp pressing cloth) before attaching the sleeves so the blocks will lie correctly when the garment is worn. The entrelac will flatten out over time as the sweater is worn.

Neckband: With larger circular, pick up and knit 60 (70, 72, 78, 80, 84) sts around the neck. BO with I-cord BO (see page 16).

Weave in all ends neatly on WS.

HAT
This hat goes well with the Twins pullover. Adjust the sizing by changing gauge.

SKILL LEVEL: Experienced
SIZES: 4-6 (8-14) years
MATERIALS
Yarn:
  CYCA #3 (DK, light worsted) Tinde Pelsullgarn from Hillesvåg (100% Norwegian wool, 284 yd/260 m / 100 g)
Yarn Colors and Amounts:
  Petroleum 652105 OR Denim Blue 65211350: 50 (50) g
Needles:
U. S. sizes 2.5 (6) / 3 (4) mm: short circular
GAUGE
22 sts in St st on larger needles = 4 in / 10 cm. Adjust needle size to obtain correct gauge if necessary.

You can adjust the hat size by changing needle size/ gauge. CO 80 sts. Work in k2, p2 ribbing for 1¼ in / 3 cm. Knit 1 rnd, decreasing evenly spaced around to 70 sts. Begin entrelac on the next round. Work 1 tier with 10 horizontal half blocks leaning from right to left, with 7 sts in each block. Work 5 tiers of whole blocks, alternating direction of blocks every tier. Finish with a "star" finishing (see page 15). Weave in all ends neatly on WS.

"Really, all you need to become a good knitter are wool, needles, hands, and slightly below-average intelligence. Of course superior intelligence, such as yours and mine, is an advantage."

ELIZABETH ZIMMERMANN,
KNITTING WITHOUT TEARS
(CHARLES SCRIBNER'S SONS, 1971)

Myrtle

This delightful dress was knitted in the round up to the armholes and then divided for front and back. The yoke is worked back and forth in entrelac. The lower edge also features entrelac, while the neck is finished with an I-cord bind-off.

DRESS

SKILL LEVEL: Experienced
SIZES: 2 (4, 6, 8) years
FINISHED MEASUREMENTS
Chest: 22 (24, 26, 27½) in / 56 (61, 66, 70) cm
Total Length: 19¾ (21¾, 23¾, 25½) in /
50 (55, 60, 65) cm
MATERIALS
Yarn:
  CYCA #3 (DK, light worsted) Tinde Pelsullgarn from
  Hillesvåg (100% Norwegian wool, 284 yd/260 m /
  100 g)
Yarn Color and Amounts:
  Pink 652110: 200 (300, 300, 400) g
Needles:
  U. S. sizes 4 and 6 / 3.5 and 4 mm: circulars
GAUGE
22 sts in St st on larger needles = 4 in / 10 cm.
Adjust needle size to obtain correct gauge if
necessary.

Body

With smaller circular and elastic cast-on (see page
16), CO 110 (125, 145, 155) sts. Join, being careful not
to twist sts; pm for beginning of rnd. Work around in
entrelac: Work 1 tier with 22 (25, 29, 31) horizontal
half blocks leaning from right to left, with 5 sts in
each block. Now work 2 tiers of whole blocks and
then 1 tier horizontal half blocks. Make sure each tier
leans in the direction opposite the previous one.

Knit 1 rnd over all the sts and, *at the same time*,
increase evenly spaced around to 144 (168, 192, 216)
sts. Change to larger circular and work around in St
st until piece measures 15 (17¼, 19, 20½) in / 38 (44,
48, 52) cm. Now (k2tog) around = 72 (84, 96, 108)
sts rem. Divide the body evenly for front and back =
36 (42, 48, 54) sts each.

Back

Now work back and forth in entrelac. Work 1 tier of
6 (7, 8, 9) horizontal half blocks leaning from right to
left, with 6 sts in each block. Pick up and knit 1 extra
st between the last st of back and first st of front and
work 1 vertical half block. The extra st is an edge st
for the vertical half block and remains an edge st as
you work up. Knit 1 tier of whole blocks from left
to right. Pick up and knit 1 extra st between the last

st of back and 1st st of front and work 1 vertical half
block on this side also. The extra st is an edge st for
the vertical half block and remains an edge st as you
work up.

Continue with whole blocks and, at each side,
vertical half blocks until you have a total of 5 (6, 6,
7) tiers of whole blocks. End with 1 tier of horizontal
half blocks. Place the 24 (24, 30, 30) center sts on a
holder for back neck.

BO shoulders loosely, but, *at the same time*, M1 after
every 3rd st; BO new sts in sequence. This technique
produces an elastic edge.

Front

Work front as for back until there are 4 (5, 5, 6) tiers,
including the first tier of horizontal half blocks. On
the next tier, work as shown on the schematic and
as detailed below.
NOTE: Place the sts of the horizontal half blocks on
a holder.

Tier 5 (6, 6, 7):
Size 2 years: Work 1 vertical half block, 1 whole
block, 2 horizontal half blocks, 1 whole block, and 1
vertical half block.
Size 4 years: Work 1 vertical half block, 2 whole
blocks, 2 horizontal half blocks, 2 whole blocks, and
1 vertical half block.
Size 6 years: Work 1 vertical half block, 2 whole
blocks, 3 horizontal half blocks, 2 whole blocks, and
1 vertical half block.
Size 8 years: Work 3 whole blocks, 3 horizontal half
blocks, and 3 whole blocks.

Work each shoulder separately.

Left Shoulder
Tier 6 (7, 7, 8):
Size 2 years: Work 1 horizontal half block.
Size 4 years: Work 2 whole blocks.
Size 6 years: Work 2 whole blocks.
Size 8 years: Work 1 vertical half block and 2 whole
blocks.

Tier – (8, 8, 9):
Size 2 years: Shoulder finished with tier 6.
Size 4 years: Work 1 quarter block and 1 horizontal
half block.
Size 6 years: Work 1 quarter block and 1 horizontal
half block.

Size 8 years: Work 2 horizontal half blocks.
Loosely BO as for back.

Right Shoulder
Work as for left shoulder but in reverse to match.

Finishing
Seam shoulders inside first stitch loops.

Neckband: With larger circular, pick up and knit 60
(60, 72, 72) sts around the neck. BO with I-cord BO
(see page 16).

Weave in all ends neatly on WS.

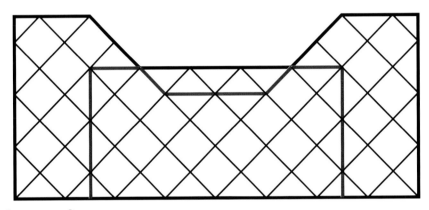

6 years   2 years

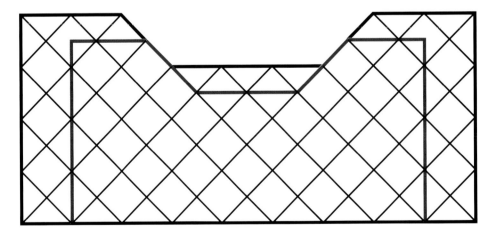

8 years   4 years

Knits for Women

We like to demonstrate that entrelac can be worn by anyone. The possibilities for variation are endless. You can feature entrelac all over a garment, or use it as a design element; work with one color or several; knit pullovers, cardigans, shawls, or skirts—just let your imagination run free. Sources of inspiration abound. Sometimes the yarn itself will give you an idea, or you'll be thinking of a TV series, or nature, or just find yourself curious as to how some particular garment could be made with entrelac. In this section of the book, you'll find items inspired by the 1980s, by cardigan knitting traditions, and by the latest fashions. Every taste can be satisfied. Garments knitted with entrelac have the advantage of being very elastic, so they fit flatteringly on the body.

Heather

We had two objectives for this shawl—to give it an old-fashioned appeal, and to make any shape but a triangle. This shawl is worked from the top down, so if you want a substantial shawl to wrap up in, you can continue knitting down to the point to eventually shape a triangle. Just remember to buy enough extra yarn.

SHAWL

SKILL LEVEL: Experienced
SIZE: One size
FINISHED MEASUREMENTS
Approx. 86½ x 13¾ in / 220 x 35 cm
MATERIALS
Yarn:
   CYCA #1 (fingering) Drops Delight from Garnstudio
   (75% wool, 25% nylon, 191 yd/175 m / 50 g)
Yarn Color and Amount:
   Beige/Gray/Pink 05: 250 g
Needles:
   U. S. size 4 / 3.5 mm: long circular
Crochet Hook:
   U. S. size E-4 / 3.5 mm
GAUGE
23 sts in St st = 4 in / 10 cm.
Adjust needle size to obtain correct gauge if necessary.

CO 420 sts. Knit 1 row, decreasing every 5th st = 350 sts
rem. Work 1 tier with 35 horizontal half blocks leaning
from right to left, with 10 sts in each block. Now work
12 tiers of whole blocks, changing direction of blocks
each tier. On the last block of every tier, BO loosely so
there will be 2 fewer blocks every tier. End with 1 tier
of horizontal half blocks, with a total of 22 blocks or 220
sts. Purl 1 row, increasing evenly spaced across to 276
sts. BO loosely. Work 1 row of single crochet on each
short side of the shawl. Weave in all ends neatly on WS.

Hynne

Hynne has buttons along one side so it can be worn many different ways. The yarn is fine and light for a lofty and comfortable poncho. It's knitted back and forth on the diagonal, with edge stitches framing the garment prettily.

CO 120 sts. Purl 1 row, *at the same time* decreasing 20 sts evenly spaced across = 100 sts rem. Work back and forth in entrelac with the first 5 and last 5 sts throughout in St st together with the vertical half blocks. At the left side, make the buttonholes in the edge sts between the vertical blocks (see schematic below). Make the buttonholes over sts 2 and 3: BO the 2nd and 3rd sts when working towards the left and then CO 2 new sts over the gap on the next row.

Work the entrelac as follows:
Begin with 5 sts of St st (edge sts), work 1 tier of 9 horizontal half blocks, with 10 sts in each block, end with 1 vertical half block, and 5 sts of St st. Work 35 tiers of whole blocks, alternating tiers of right-leaning and left-leaning blocks, with vertical half blocks at the sides. Make 7 buttonholes on the first half of the garment (see schematic). End with 1 tier of horizontal half blocks. Knit 1 row over all sts, increasing evenly spaced across to 120 sts. BO loosely; weave in all ends neatly on WS.

Sew buttons on the same side of the piece as the buttonholes, but on the second half.

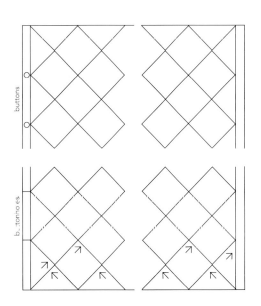

PONCHO/SHAWL

SKILL LEVEL: Experienced
SIZE: One size
FINISHED MEASUREMENTS
Approx. 30 x 63 in / 76 x 160 cm
MATERIALS
Yarn:
   CYCA #4 (worsted, afghan, Aran) Drops Alpaca Silk Brushed from Garnstudio (77% alpaca, 23% silk, 153 yd/140 m / 25 g)
Yarn Color and Amount:
   Light Gray 02: 200 g
Other Materials:
   7 buttons, approx. ¾ in / 20 mm in diameter
Needles:
   U. S. size 8 / 5 mm: long and short circulars
GAUGE
23 sts in St st = 4 in / 10 cm.
Adjust needle size to obtain correct gauge if necessary.

Drift

PELSWOOL PONCHO AND COWL SET

This poncho features a wide section of entrelac down the center front and back. The poncho is worked from the bottom up, back and forth in two pieces and later seamed at the sides. The poncho is paired with a cowl for extra warmth on cold days.

PONCHO

SKILL LEVEL: Experienced
SIZE: One size
FINISHED MEASUREMENTS
Total Length: approx. 39½ in / 100 cm
MATERIALS
Yarn: CYCA #5 (bulky) Blåne Pelsullgarn from Hifa
   (100% wool, 125 yd/114 m / 100 g)
Yarn Color and Amount:
   Natural Gray 672115: 900 g
Needles:
   U. S. size 10 / 6 mm: long circular
GAUGE
14 sts in St st = 4 in / 10 cm.
Adjust needle size to obtain correct gauge if
necessary.

Front

Using elastic cast-on method (see page 16), CO 27
sts.
K1, p3 (these 3 sts are purled on RS, which should
always be facing you), k1 (edge st), work 3
horizontal half blocks leaning from right to left, with
6 sts in each block, k1 (edge st), p3 (these 3 sts are
purled on RS, which should always be facing you),
yo, k1.
Next row: K1, k1tbl (with yarnover of previous row),
p3, work 1 vertical half block on left side of work, 2
whole blocks leaning from left to right, 1 vertical half
block on right side of work, p3, yo, k to end of row.

Continue as est, increasing on each side of the piece
until there are 17 tiers of whole blocks (including the
horizontal half blocks at the beginning of the work)
or until piece measures approx. 19¾ in / 50 cm.
Increases are worked with a yarnover inside the last
st of each row. Always work yarnover as a twisted st
on the following row.

Now continue the piece as est, *but* decrease with
k2tog inside the last st of each row. When there
are a total of 27 tiers of whole blocks (including the
horizontal half blocks at the beginning of the piece)
or piece measures approx. 31½ in / 80 cm, bind off
for the neck.

Neck

On the next tier, work 3 horizontal half blocks
leaning from right to left and then continue as est to
end of row. Place the horizontal half block sts on a
holder. Work each side of neck separately.
Left side: Work back and forth in St st and, *at the
same time*, decrease 1 st inside last st of the row, on
both left and right sides of row. Work until 1 st rem.
Place sts on a holder.

Right side: Work mirror-image to left side.

Back

The back is worked without shaping up to the neck.
Work as for front until back has 31 tiers of whole
blocks (including horizontal half blocks). Work 1 tier
of horizontal half blocks and complete row. There
should be 8 sts on each side of the horizontal blocks.
Place sts from the half blocks on a holder together
with the 8 sts on each side of the blocks.

Finishing

Seam the front and back pieces from the point and
up to the sts on holder. Slide sts from holder onto
short circular and pick up and knit sts from each side
of neck as follows:
From back: 9 sts + sts of half blocks (3 x 6 sts) + 9
sts + 1 st from front + pick up and knit 8 sts from St
st section + sts from half blocks (3 x 6 sts) + pick up
and knit 8 sts from St st section + 1 st = 72 sts total.
Work in k2, p2 ribbing for ¾ in / 2 cm. BO loosely.
Weave in all ends neatly on WS.

COWL

SKILL LEVEL: Experienced
SIZE: One size
FINISHED MEASUREMENTS
Length: approx. 6¼ in / 16 cm
Circumference: approx. 25¼ in / 64 cm
MATERIALS
Yarn:
   CYCA #5 (bulky) Blåne Pelsullgarn from Hifa
   (100% wool, 125 yd/114 m / 100 g)
Yarn Color and Amount:
   Natural Gray 672115: 100 g
Needles:
   U. S. size 10 / 6 mm: circular
GAUGE
14 sts in St st = 4 in / 10 cm.
Adjust needle size to obtain correct gauge if
   necessary.

Using elastic cast-on method (see page 16), CO 66 sts. Work 1 tier with 11 horizontal half blocks leaning from left to right, with 6 sts in each block. Work 4 tiers of whole blocks that alternate direction of leaning each tier. Finish with 1 tier of horizontal half blocks. BO loosely, but, *at the same time*, M1 after every 3rd st; BO new sts in sequence. This technique produces an elastic edge. Weave in all ends neatly on WS.

" Life should be like knitting: you can rip out and begin again when there are mistakes. "

SOURCE UNKNOWN

Hege

PULLOVER AND HAT

Hege is a Norwegian first name. Here's a sweater that is amazingly soft and has a beautiful relaxed fit. The sweater is knitted in the round up to the armholes and then divided for front and back with each then separately knit back and forth. The sleeves are sewn in without a facing at the sleeve top. The entrelac is very elastic, so garment measurements are approximate. The blocks are knitted with paired yarns for a distinctive structural effect. You can easily adjust the garment length with more or fewer tiers of whole blocks. Doubled yarn is used throughout: 1 strand Alpaca + 1 strand Baby Alpaca Silk, or 1 strand each Alpaca and Alpaca Silk Brushed.

The one-size hat (see page 103) is rather slouchy. We added a fake fur pompom attached with a snap so you can easily wash the hat.

PULLOVER

SKILL LEVEL: Experienced
SIZES: XS (S, M, L, XL, XXL)
FINISHED MEASUREMENTS
Chest: 34¾ (38½, 43, 47¼, 51½, 56) in / 88 (98, 109, 120, 131, 142) cm
Total Length: 20½ (22¾, 24¾, 31, 34, 36¼) in / 52 (58, 63, 79, 86, 92) cm
Sleeve Length: 18¼ (17¾, 17¼, 17, 16½, 16½) in / 46 (45, 44, 43, 42, 42) cm
MATERIALS
Yarns:
  CYCA #2 (sport, baby) Drops Alpaca from Garnstudio (100% alpaca, 183 yd/167 m / 50 g)
  CYCA #2 (sport, baby) Drops Baby Alpaca Silk from Garnstudio (70% alpaca, 30% silk, 183 yd/167 m / 50 g
  CYCA #4 (worsted, afghan, Aran) Drops Alpaca Silk Brushed from Garnstudio (77% alpaca, 23% silk, 153 yd/140 m / 25 g)
Yarn Colors and Amounts:
  Drops Alpaca: Natural 100: 300 (350, 350, 400, 400, 400) g
  Drops Baby Alpaca Silk: Natural 0100: 150 (150, 200, 200, 200, 200) g
  Drops Alpaca Silk Brushed: Natural 01: 100 (100, 150, 150, 200, 200) g
Needles:
  U. S. sizes 6 and 8 / 4 and 5 mm: circular and set of 5 dpn
GAUGE
17 sts in St st on larger needles = 4 in / 10 cm. Adjust needle size to obtain correct gauge if necessary.

Body
With smaller circular and holding a strand each of Alpaca and Baby Alpaca Silk, CO 148 (168, 186, 204, 210, 226) sts. Join, being careful not to twist cast-on row; pm for beginning of rnd. Work around in k1, p1 ribbing for 1½ in / 4 cm. Change to larger circular. Knit 1 rnd decreasing evenly spaced around to 112 (126, 140, 154, 168, 182) sts. Now work entrelac in the round. Change to 1 strand each Alpaca and Alpaca Silk Brushed. Work 1 tier of 14 horizontal half blocks leaning from right to left, with 8 (9, 10, 11, 12, 13) sts in each block. Continue with tiers of whole blocks alternating tiers of 1 strand each Alpaca + Baby Alpaca Silk and 1 strand each Alpaca + Alpaca Silk Brushed. Continue until there are 6 (6, 6, 8, 8, 8) tiers, including the first tier of horizontal half blocks (or, a total of 8 tiers for all sizes if you want a longer sweater, even for the smallest size). Now divide the body for front and back with 7 blocks in each part. Work front and back separately.

Back
Now work entrelac back and forth. Work 1 tier with 7 whole blocks leaning from right to left, with 8 (9, 10, 11, 12, 13) sts in each block. This tier also has a vertical half block on each side: pick up and knit 1 extra st between the block on the front and the block on the back for an edge st on the vertical half blocks. Continue as est until there are a total of 11 (11, 11, 13, 13, 13) tiers of whole blocks. End with 1 tier of horizontal half blocks. Place the 24 (27, 30, 33, 36, 39) center sts on a holder for back neck. Work shoulders separately.

Shoulders: BO loosely, but, *at the same time*, M1 after every 3rd st; BO new sts in sequence. This technique produces an elastic edge.

Front
Work front as for back until you have a total of 10 (10, 10, 12, 12, 12) tiers of whole blocks. On the next tier, work as shown on the schematic and description below.

Tier 11 (11, 11, 13, 13, 13): Work 1 vertical half block, 2 whole blocks, 2 horizontal half blocks, 2 whole blocks, and 1 vertical half block. Place the sts of the horizontal half blocks on a holder. Now work each shoulder separately.

Left Shoulder
Work from left to right:
Tier 12 (12, 12, 14, 14, 14): Work 2 horizontal half blocks. BO as for back.

Right Shoulder
Work as for left shoulder, reversing shaping to correspond.

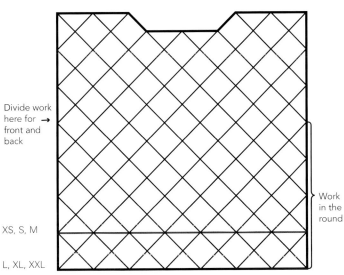

Divide work here for → front and back

Work in the round

XS, S, M

L, XL, XXL

Sleeves

The sleeves are worked in St st with 1 strand each Alpaca and Alpaca Silk Brushed held together. With smaller dpn, CO 38 (40, 42, 44, 46, 48) sts. Divide sts onto dpn and join; pm for beginning of rnd. Work around in k1, p1 ribbing for 1½ in / 4 cm. Change to larger circular. Knit 1 rnd, increasing 4 sts evenly spaced around = 42 (44, 46, 48, 50, 52) sts. Pm at center of underarm. Every ¾ in / 2 cm, increase 1 st after marker and 1 st before marker until there are 60 (66, 72, 78 84, 90) sts. Continue until sleeve is 18¼ (17¾, 17¼, 17, 16½, 16½) in / 46 (45, 44, 43, 42, 42) cm long. BO loosely. Make the second sleeve the same way.

Finishing

Seam shoulders.

Neck Band: Work with 1 strand each Alpaca and Alpaca Silk held together. With smaller short circular, place the held 16 (18, 20, 22, 24, 26) front neck sts + the held 24 (27, 30, 33, 36, 39) back neck sts on needle. Pick up and knit a total of 30 (33, 34, 37, 38, 41) sts at sides of neck = 70 (78, 84, 92, 98, 106) sts total. Work around in k1, p1 ribbing for 1¼ in / 3 cm. BO loosely in ribbing.

Attach sleeves and weave in all ends neatly on WS.

HAT

SKILL LEVEL: Experienced
SIZES: Women's, head circumference 21¾-23¾ in / 55-60 cm
MATERIALS
Yarns:
   CYCA #2 (sport, baby) Drops Alpaca from Garnstudio (100% alpaca, 183 yd/167 m / 50 g)
   CYCA #2 (sport, baby) Drops Baby Alpaca Silk from Garnstudio (70% alpaca, 30% silk, 183 yd/167 m / 50 g
   CYCA #4 (worsted, afghan, Aran) Drops Alpaca Silk Brushed from Garnstudio (77% alpaca, 23% silk, 153 yd/140 m / 25 g)
Yarn Colors and Amounts:
   Drops Alpaca: Natural 100: 50 g
   Drops Baby Alpaca Silk: Natural 0100: 50 g
   Drops Alpaca Silk Brushed: Natural 01: 50 g
Other Materials:
   1 fake fur pompom if desired
Needles:
   U. S. size 8 / 5 mm: short circular or set of 5 dpn
GAUGE
17 sts in St st = 4 in / 10 cm.
Adjust needle size to obtain correct gauge if necessary.

Holding 1 strand each Alpaca and Baby Alpaca Silk together, CO 80 sts and join; pm for beginning of rnd Work 10 rnds k2, p2 ribbing. Knit 1 rnd, decreasing evenly spaced around to 70 sts. Change to 1 strand each Alpaca and Alpaca Silk Brushed. Work 1 tier of 7 horizontal half blocks with 10 sts in each block.

Work 3 tiers of whole blocks, alternating yarn pairs of1 strand each Alpaca + Alpaca Silk and 1 strand each Alpaca + Alpaca Silk Brushed.

Finish the hat with a "star" shaping (see page 15). Weave in all ends neatly on WS. Attach a fake fur pompom by sewing or with a snap.

Livø

PULLOVER AND SKIRT

Livø is a Norwegian first name. A pretty sweater with an entrelac yoke, knitted with a mix of wool and alpaca. The sweater is worked from the bottom up, ending with the entrelac yoke.

The skirt (see page 106) is also worked from the bottom up, with the lower section in entrelac and stockinette towards the waist. A casing at the waist allows for an elastic band to ensure the skirt fits well.

SKILL LEVEL: Experienced
SIZES: XS (S, M, L, XL, XXL)
FINISHED MEASUREMENTS
Chest: 30¾ (33½, 36¼, 38½, 45¼, 47¾) in / 78 (85, 92, 98, 115, 121) cm
Total Length: 22½ (23¼, 24, 24¾, 25½, 26) in / 57 (59, 61, 63, 65, 66) cm
Sleeve Length: 17¼ (18¼, 19, 19, 18½, 18½) in / 44 (46, 48, 48, 47, 47) cm
MATERIALS
Yarns:
   CYCA #2 (sport, baby) Tumi from Rauma (50% alpaca, 50% wool, 142 yd/130 m / 50 g)
Yarn Colors and Amounts:
   Color 1: Light Gray SFN38: 300 (350, 350, 450, 500, 600) g
   Color 2: Steel Gray 1992: 50 (50, 50, 50, 50, 100) g
   Color 3: Sea Green 1244: 50 (50, 50, 50, 50, 50) g
   Color 4: Petroleum 6396: 50 (50, 50, 50, 50, 50) g
   Color 5: Navy Blue 6416: 50 (50, 50, 50, 50, 50) g
   Color 6: Countryside Blue 0190: 50 (50, 50, 50, 50, 50) g
   Color 7: Light Blue 1647: 50 (50, 50, 50, 50, 50) g
Needles:
   U. S. sizes 2.5 and 4 / 3 and 3.5 mm: circulars and sets of 5 dpn
GAUGE
24 sts in St st on larger needles = 4 in / 10 cm
Adjust needle size to obtain correct gauge if necessary.

Body
With smaller circular and Color 1, CO 188 (204, 220, 236, 276, 290) sts. Join, being careful not to twist cast-on row; pm for beginning of rnd. Work around in k2, p2 ribbing for 1½ in / 4 cm. Pm marker at each side = 94 (102, 110, 118, 138, 145) sts each for front and back. Change to larger circular and work in St st until body measures 16½ (17¼, 17¾, 18¼, 18¼, 18¼) in / 42 (44, 45, 46, 46, 46) cm. BO 5 sts on each side of each marker for underarms. Set body aside while you work the sleeves.

Sleeves
With smaller dpn and Color 1, CO 44 (46, 48, 50, 52, 54) sts. Divide sts onto dpn and join; pm for beginning of rnd. Work around in k2, p2 ribbing for 1½ in / 4 cm. Change to larger dpn and work in St st. *At the same time*, increase 1 st at each side of marker every ⅝ (⅝, ⅝, ¾, ¾, ¾) in / 1.5 (1.5, 1.5, 2, 2, 2) cm to a total of 82 (86, 90, 94, 98, 102) sts.

Continue in St st until sleeve is 17¼ (18¼, 19, 19, 18½, 18½) in / 44 (46, 48, 48, 47, 47) cm long or desired length. BO 10 sts centered at underarm. Set sleeve aside and make a second one the same way.

Yoke
Place the body and sleeve sts on *smaller* circular = 312 (336, 360, 384, 432, 454) sts total. With Color 1, knit 1 rnd, decreasing evenly spaced around to 187 (198, 216, 234, 252, 270) sts. We recommend using the smaller circular so the transition from St st to entrelac will be as smooth as possible. Now change to larger circular and work around in entrelac. The rnd begins at center back (pm here) so the blocks will be arranged symmetrically in relation to the sleeves.

Tier 1, with Color 1: Work 17 (18, 18, 18, 18, 18) horizontal half blocks leaning from right to left, with 11 (11, 12, 13, 14, 15) sts in each block.
Tier 2, with Color 2: Work whole blocks leaning from left to right, with 11 (11, 12, 13, 14, 15) sts in each block.
Tier 3, with Color 3: Work whole blocks leaning from right to left, with 9 (9, 10, 11, 12, 13) sts in each block.
Tier 4, with Color 4: Work whole blocks leaning from left to right, with 7 (7, 8, 9, 10, 11) sts in each block.
Tier 5, with Color 5: Work whole blocks leaning from right to left, with 6 (6, 6, 7, 8, 9) sts in each block.
Tier 6, with Color 6: Work whole blocks leaning from left to right, with 5 (5, 5, 6, 7, 8) sts in each block.
Tier 7, with Color 7: Work whole blocks leaning from right to left, with 4 (4, 4, 5, 6, 6) sts in each block.
Tier 8, with Color 1: Work 1 tier of horizontal half blocks leaning from left to right, with 4 (4, 4, 5, 5, 6) sts in each block.
Now 68 (72, 72, 90, 90, 108) sts rem. Knit 1 rnd, increasing evenly spaced around to 88 (82, 96, 100, 112 120) sts. Change to smaller circular and work around in k2, p2 ribbing for 1½ in / 4 cm. BO loosely in ribbing.

Finishing
Seam underarms. Weave in all ends neatly on WS.

SKIRT

SKILL LEVEL: Experienced
SIZES: XS (S, M, L, XL, XXL)
FINISHED MEASUREMENTS
Circumference at Waist: 22¾ (23¾, 26, 28¼, 33, 35½) in / 58 (60, 66, 72, 84, 90) cm (measured flat without stretching)
Total Length: 16½ (17¾, 17¾, 19, 20½, 20½) in / 42 (45, 45, 48, 52, 52) cm
Circumference around Lower Edge: 34¼ (35½, 39½, 42½, 47¼, 51¼) in / 87 (90, 100, 108, 120, 130) cm
MATERIALS
Yarns:
CYCA #2 (sport, baby) Tumi from Rauma
(50% alpaca, 50% wool, 142 yd/130 m / 50 g)
Yarn Colors and Amounts:
Color 1: Light Gray SFN38: 200 (250, 250, 250, 300, 300) g
Color 2: Steel Gray 1992: 50 (50, 50, 50, 50, 100) g
Color 3: Sea Green 1244: 50 (50, 50, 50, 50, 50) g
Color 4: Petroleum 6396: 50 (50, 50, 50, 50, 50) g
Color 5: Navy Blue 6416: 50 (50, 50, 50, 50, 50) g
Color 6: Countryside Blue 0190: 50 (50, 50, 50, 50, 50) g
Color 7: Light Blue 1647: 50 (50, 50, 50, 50, 50) g
Other Materials:
Waistband elastic—long enough to encircle waist + seam allowance at each end.
Needles:
U. S. size 2.5 / 3 mm: circular
GAUGE
24 sts in St st = 4 in / 10 cm.
Adjust needle size to obtain correct gauge if necessary.

With Color 1, CO 208 (216, 240, 260, 288, 312) sts. Join, being careful not to twist cast-on row; pm for beginning of rnd. Knit 1 rnd, decreasing 78 (76, 86, 92, 96, 108) sts evenly spaced around = 130 (140, 154, 168, 192, 204) sts rem. Work 1 tier with 13 (14, 14, 14, 16, 17) horizontal half blocks leaning from left to right, with 10 (10, 11, 12, 12, 12) sts in each block. Work a total of 6 tiers of whole blocks, changing color (in sequence above) and alternate direction of blocks each tier. End with 1 tier of horizontal half blocks in Color 1. On the next rnd, knit all the sts and, *at the same time*, increase evenly spaced around to 208 (216, 240, 260, 288, 312) sts.

On the next rnd, pm as follows: K26 (27, 30, 33, 36, 39), pm, k52 (54, 60, 65, 72, 78), pm, k52 (54, 60, 65, 72, 78), pm, k52 (54, 60, 65, 72, 78), pm, knit to end of rnd. At each side of each marker, decrease as follows: On left side of marker, k2tog, on right side of marker, k2tog tbl.

Continue in St st and, *at the same time*, decrease as described above every 1 (1, ¾, 1, 1, 1¼) in / 2.5 (2.5, 2, 2.5, 2.5, 3) cm a total of 9 (9, 10, 11, 11, 12) times = 136 (144, 160, 172, 200, 216) sts rem. Now continue in St st without decreasing until skirt is 16½ (17¾, 17¾, 19, 20½, 20½) in / 42 (45, 45, 48, 52, 52) cm long. Purl 1 rnd for the foldline and then knit 4 rnds. On the next rnd, BO 4 sts for the casing and then knit to end of rnd. On the next rnd, CO 4 sts over the bound-off sts. Knit 5 rnds and then BO loosely.

Finishing
Turn casing down at purl foldline and sew down, making sure it is not too tight. Draw elastic through casing and seam. Weave in all ends neatly on WS.

Mountain Rose

The Mountain Rose cardigan is worked from the top down, making it easy to adjust the length of the body and sleeves. The entrelac yoke is worked back and forth and then the body is worked in the round with a steek. Because the sweater is knitted with Finullgarn, you can cut the steek open without having to reinforce it first. The cut edges are covered with a knitted facing. The sleeves are knitted down from the armholes so there are no seams to sew!

CARDIGAN

SKILL LEVEL: Experienced
SIZES: XS (S, M, L, XL, XXL)
FINISHED MEASUREMENTS
Chest: 29½ (33½, 36¾, 39½, 45¼, 48) in / 75 (85, 93, 100, 115, 122) cm
Total Length: 22½ (23¼, 24, 24¾, 25½, 26) in / 57 (59, 61, 63, 65, 66) cm
Sleeve Length: 17¾ (18¼, 18½, 19, 19¼, 19¼) in / 45 (46, 47, 48, 49, 49) cm
MATERIALS
Yarns:
CYCA #1 (fingering) Finull PT2 from Rauma (100% wool, 191 yd/175 m / 50 g)
Yarn Colors and Amounts:
Color 1: Gray 404: 300 (300, 350, 400, 450, 500) g
Color 2: Apple Green 498: 50 (50, 50, 50, 50, 50) g
Color 3: Yellow-Green 417: 50 (50, 50, 50, 50, 50) g
Color 4: Golden Brown 4076: 50 (50, 50, 50, 50, 50) g
Color 5: Burnt Orange 434: 50 (50, 50, 50, 50, 50) g
Color 6: Rust Red 419 0190: 50 (50, 50, 50, 50, 50) g
Color 7: Red Brown 428: 50 (50, 50, 50, 50, 50) g
Color 8: Burgundy 470: 50 (50, 50, 50, 50, 100) g
Other Materials:
8-9 hook and clasp sets (see photos for style of clasp)
Needles:
U. S. size 2.5 / 3 mm: 24 and 32 in / 60 and 80 cm circulars and sets of 5 dpn. For sizes XS and S, you'll also need dpn U. S. size 1.5 / 2.5 mm

GAUGE
24 sts in St st on larger needles = 4 in / 10 cm.
Adjust needle size to obtain correct gauge if necessary.

Yoke

Allow for 1 edge st at each side. This is indicated with +2 in the stitch counts. Using elastic cast-on method (see page 16), Color 2, and short circular U. S. size 2.5 / 3 mm, CO 68+2 (72+2, 72+2, 90+2, 95+2, 95+2) sts. Make sure the cast-on is not too tight.

Tier 1 with Color 2: Work 17 (18, 18, 18, 19, 19) horizontal half blocks leaning from right to left, with 4 (4, 4, 5, 5, 5) sts in each block. Do not knit the edge st at each side—they will be used for the vertical half blocks in the next tier. Continue in Color 2.

Tier 2, with Color 2: Work whole blocks leaning from left to right, with 4 (4, 4, 5, 5, 5) sts in each block. Make 1 vertical half block at each side. Change to Color 3 in the last vertical half block as follows: When 3 sts rem on left needle, sl 1, change to Color 3, complete row. Sl first st, sl next st, work next st and psso. Tier 2 is now complete.

Tier 3, with Color 3: Work whole blocks leaning from right to left, with 5 (5, 5, 6, 6, 6) sts in each block. Work edge st after last whole block of the tier with Color 4.

Tier 4, with Color 4: Work whole blocks leaning from left to right, with 6 (6, 6, 7, 7, 7) sts in each block. Make 1 vertical half block at each side. Change to Color 5 in the last vertical half block as follows: When 3 sts rem on left needle, sl 1, change to Color 5, complete row. Sl first st, sl next st, work next st and psso. Tier 4 is now complete.

Tier 5, with Color 5: Work whole blocks leaning from right to left, with 7 (7, 8, 9, 9, 9) sts in each block. Work edge st after last whole block of the tier with Color 6.

Tier 6, with Color 6: Work whole blocks leaning from left to right, with 9 (9, 10, 11, 11, 11) sts in each block. Make 1 vertical half block at each side. Change to Color 7 in the last vertical half block as follows: When 3 sts rem on left needle, sl 1, change to Color 7, complete row. Sl first st, sl next st, work next st and psso. Tier 6 is now complete.

Tier 7, with Color 7: Work whole blocks leaning from right to left, with 10 (10, 11, 12, 13, 13) sts in each block. Work edge st after last whole block of the tier with Color 8.

Tier 8, with Color 8: Work whole blocks leaning from left to right, with 11 (11, 12, 13, 14, 15) sts in each block. Make 1 vertical half block at each side. Change to Color 1 in the last vertical half block as follows: When 3 sts rem on left needle, sl 1, change to Color 1, complete row. Sl first st, sl next st, work next st and psso. Tier 8 is now complete.

Tier 9, with Color 1: Work horizontal half blocks leaning from right to left, with 11 (11, 12, 13, 14, 15) sts in each block.

There are now 187+2 (198+2, 216+2, 234+2, 266+2, 285+2) sts. From this point on, the cardigan is worked in the round. CO 5 new sts at center front for the steek. These sts are always purled and indicated by +5. Continue the body in St st. On the first rnd, M1 between each st (except for the 5 steek sts) to avoid holes in the transition from entrelac to St st. This extra effort is well worth the trouble. On the next rnd, decrease evenly spaced around to 304+5 (336+5, 364+5, 388+5, 432+5, 456+5) sts.

On the next rnd, divide body and sleeves: K40 (46, 51, 55, 64, 68), place next 72 (76, 80, 84, 88, 92) sts on a holder for first sleeve; CO 10 sts for underarm. K80 (92, 102, 110, 128, 136), place next 72 (76, 80, 84, 88, 92) sts on a holder for second sleeve; CO 10 sts for underarm. K40 (46, 51, 55, 64, 68) + p5.

Body

The body now has 180+5 (204+5, 224+5, 240+5, 276+5, 292+5) sts. Continue in St st with Color 1 for 11½ (12¼, 12¼, 12¼, 12¾) in / 29 (31, 31, 31, 31, 32) cm as measured down from the transition row

between entrelac and St st. Knit 1 rnd, *at the same time*, decreasing 60 (72, 74, 84, 96, 100) sts evenly spaced around (do not decrease within steek) = 120 (132, 150, 156, 180, 192) sts rem.

Lower Edge in Entrelac

BO the 5 steek sts and work back and forth in entrelac. See the yoke instructions for changing colors.

Tier 1, with Color 1: Work 20 (22, 25, 26, 30, 32) horizontal half blocks leaning from right to left, with 6 sts in each block. Pick up and knit 1 st at each side of work for edge sts.

Tier 2, with Color 6: Work whole blocks leaning from left to right, and a vertical half block at each side.

Tier 3, with Color 7: Work whole blocks leaning from right to left.

Tier 4, with Color 8: Work whole blocks leaning from left to right and a vertical half block at each side.

Tier 5, with Color 1: Work horizontal half blocks leaning from right to left.

BO loosely, but, *at the same time*, M1 after every 3rd

" To leave your fingers untrained for anything beyond pushing, and perhaps twisting, is like leaving a voice without singing. It is a shame and a loss. Certainly knitting is not the only thing that fingers can do but it is a good thing: simple, yet capable of endless complexity. "

ANNA ZILBOORG,
KNITTING FOR ANARCHISTS (DOVER, 2002)

st; BO new sts in sequence. This technique produces an elastic edge.

Sleeves

Slip held sts for one sleeve to larger needle, CO 10 sts for underarm (pm at center of these sts = beginning of rnd) = 82 (86 90, 94, 98, 102) sts total. With Color 1, work around in St st. When sleeve measures ¾ in / 2 cm from transition from entrelac to St st, decrease 1 st on each side of marker. Rep the decreases every ¾ (¾, ¾, ¾, ⅝, ⅝) in / 2 (2, 2, 2, 1.5, 1.5) cm a total of 19 (20, 21, 22, 23, 24) times = 44 (46, 48, 50, 52, 54) sts rem.
When sleeve measures 15 (15½, 15¾, 16¼, 16¼, 16¼) in / 38 (39, 40, 41, 41, 41) cm, knit 1 rnd, *at the same time* decreasing 8 (10, 12, 14, 10, 12) sts evenly spaced around = 36 (36, 36, 36, 42, 42) sts rem.

Entrelac Cuff

Change to needles U.S. 1.5 (1.5, 2.5, 2.5, 2.5, 2.5) / 2.5 (2.5, 3, 3, 3, 3) mm.
Tier 1, with Color 1: Work with 6 (6, 6, 6, 7, 7) horizontal half blocks leaning from right to left, with 6 sts in each block.
Tier 2, with Color 6: Work whole blocks leaning from left to right.

Tier 3, with Color 7: Work whole blocks leaning from right to left.
Tier 4, with Color 8: Work whole blocks leaning from left to right.
Tier 5, with Color 1: Work horizontal half blocks leaning from right to left.

BO loosely, but, *at the same time* M1 after every 3rd st; BO new sts in sequence. This technique produces an elastic edge.

Finishing

Carefully cut steek open down center st. With Finull yarn, you should not need to reinforce before cutting. However, if you knitted the sweater with a different yarn type, such alpaca or superwash, machine-stitch down each side of the center steek st before cutting.

Pick up and knit sts (about 3 sts for every 4 rows) along the edge between the St st and cut edge. Make a St st facing about 1¼-1½ in / 3-4 cm wide and BO. Fold the facing over the cut edge and sew down.

Sew on 8-9 clasps evenly spaced down front edge.

Embla

LOVELY LONG JACKET

In Norse mythology, Embla was the name of the first human woman created by the gods. The back and two front sections of this jacket are each worked separately, back and forth. The front bands are worked as part of each front, with buttonholes on the right band. The sleeves are worked in the round in entrelac and shaped by gradually adding stitches to the entrelac blocks.

SKILL LEVEL: Experienced
SIZES: XS (S, M, L, XL, XXL)
FINISHED MEASUREMENTS
Chest: 45¾ (47¼, 52½, 54¾, 59¾, 65¼) in / 116 (120, 133, 139, 152, 166) cm
Total Length: 27½ (29½, 31½, 33, 35½, 37¾) in / 70 (75, 80, 84, 90, 96) cm
Sleeve Length: 16¼ (16½, 17, 17, 17, 17¼) in / 41 (42, 43, 43, 43, 44) cm
MATERIALS
Yarn: CYCA #3 (DK, light worsted) Tinde Pelsullgarn from Hillesvåg (100% Norwegian wool, 284 yd/ 260 m / 100 g)
Yarn Color and Amount:
    Burgundy 652104: 600 (650, 650, 700, 700, 750) g
Other Materials:
    Buttons (as many as buttonholes made for your size)
Needles:
    U. S. size 6 / 4 mm: circular and set of 5 dpn,
GAUGE
22 sts in St st = 4 in / 10 cm.
Adjust needle size to obtain correct gauge if necessary.

Back
With circular and using elastic cast-on method (see page 16), CO 82 (90, 98, 102, 112, 122) sts. The first and last sts are edge sts and worked with the vertical half blocks.

Knit 1 tier of 8 (8, 8, 10, 10, 10) horizontal half blocks leaning from right to left, with 10 (11, 12, 10, 11, 12) sts in each block. Work 17 (17, 17, 19, 19, 19) tiers of whole blocks, alternating direction of blocks on each tier. Finish with 1 tier of horizontal half blocks. Place the sts of the center 4 half blocks on a holder for back neck. BO shoulder sts loosely, but, *at the same time*, M1 after every 3rd st; BO new sts in sequence. This technique produces an elastic edge. Set back aside.

Front
With circular and using elastic cast-on method (see page 16), CO 48 (52, 56, 58, 63, 68) sts. The first 7 sts form the front band which is worked together with the vertical half blocks. Work these 7 sts as k1, p1 ribbing. On the right front, work buttonholes over the center 3 sts of the band. For each buttonhole: BO 3 sts and, on next row, CO 3 sts over gap, between each vertical half block along entire front. The last st (or, the first st on left front) is an edge st for a smoother edge.

Work 1 tier with 4 (4, 4, 5, 5, 5) horizontal half blocks leaning from right to left, with 10 (11, 12, 10, 11, 12) sts in each block. Work 13 (13, 13, 15, 15, 15) tiers of whole blocks, alternating direction on each tier. Place the front band sts on a holder (the rest of the band will be worked later). Now work 1 block less at neck edge on each tier instead of working vertical half blocks. Work 1 extra row on these blocks to avoid cutting the yarn each time. Place all the sts

L   XS
XL   S
XXL   M

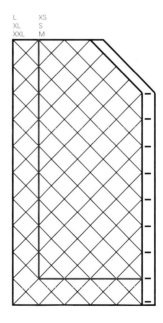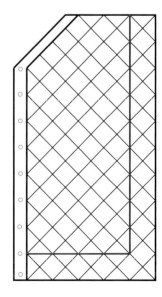

▬ = Buttonhole
○ = Button

Tier Number	XS	S	M	L	XL	XXL
1	5	6	7	5	6	7
2	5	6	7	5	6	7
3	5	7	7	6	7	8
4	6	7	8	6	7	8
5	6	8	8	7	8	8
6	7	8	9	7	8	9
7	7	9	9	7	9	9
8	8	9	9	8	9	10
9	8	9	10	8	10	10
10	8	10	10	8	10	11
11	9	10	10	9	10	11
12	9	10	11	9	11	11
13	9	11	11	9	11	12
14	10	11	12	10	11	12
15	10	11	12	10	11	12
16	10			10		
17	10			10		

work entrelac in the round following the table. There should be 5 (5, 5, 6, 6, 6) blocks in each tier. The table shows the number of sts per block in the various tiers. The first and last tier consists of horizontal half blocks.

After completing all the tiers, work 1 rnd st over all the sts, *at the same time* increasing evenly spaced around to 87 (96, 105, 106, 110, 120) sts. BO loosely.

Finishing
Seam shoulders.

Neckband
Place the sts of one front band on needle and work the band around the neck as follows: Work all the sts of the band except last st. Place the band with the diagonal edge on the front, pick up the yarn in the outermost stitch loop of the front, place the new st on needle with band, work last st and new st tog. Turn work and complete row. Each time you work at front edge, pick up 1 st and knit it tog with last st of row. When there are sts on a holder, work these sts tog with the last st of the row instead of picking up 1 new st. Continue the same way along the V-neck of the front to center of back neck.

Work the same way with band of opposite front. Join the two sets of band sts at center back neck. Attach sleeves. Weave in all ends neatly on WS.

Sew on the buttons to left front.

of the blocks leaning from left to right on a holder to be used later when the band is knitted along the V-neck. Continue until there are 17 (17, 17, 19, 19, 19) tiers of whole blocks. Finish with 1 tier of horizontal half blocks. BO the shoulder as for back. Set piece aside while you work the opposite front, reversing shaping to match.

Sleeves
The sleeves are worked in the round with entrelac and shaped by increasing the number of stitches in each block (by picking up and knitting extra stitches). Do not work more rows in the blocks even when increasing. That way, the increases are spread over 2 tiers.

With circular and using elastic cast-on method (see page 16), CO 25 (30, 35, 30, 36, 42) sts. Now

Mist

SHORT WRAP-AROUND JACKET

This jacket is a short, close-fitting wrap-around. The back and two front pieces are worked separately. The sleeves are sewn in later. The body is worked in entrelac but the sleeves are stockinette and edged with entrelac. Each front is edged with a knitted band ending with a long tie to hold the sweater around the body.

SKILL LEVEL: Experienced
SIZES: XS (S, M, L, XL, XXL)
FINISHED MEASUREMENTS
Chest: 31½ (34¾, 38½, 41¾, 46½, 54¼) in / 80 (88, 98, 106, 118, 130) cm
Total Length: 20½ (21¼, 22½, 22½, 22¾, 25½) in / 52 (54, 57, 57, 58, 65) cm
Sleeve Length: 18½ (18½, 18½, 18½, 18½, 18½) in / 47 (47, 47, 47, 47, 47) cm
MATERIALS
Yarn: CYCA #1 (fingering) Sølje from Hillesvåg (100% Norwegian wool, 383 yd/350 m / 100 g)
Yarn Color and Amount:
Olive Green 642118: 400 (400, 450, 500, 500, 550) g
Needles:
U. S. sizes 1.5 and 2.5 / 2.5 and 3 mm: circulars and sets of 5 dpn
GAUGE
25 sts in St st on larger needles = 4 in / 10 cm. Adjust needle size to obtain correct gauge if necessary.

Back

With larger circular, using elastic method (see page 16), CO 56 (64, 72, 81, 90, 100) sts. Work back and forth in entrelac as follows: Work 1 tier of 7 (8, 8, 9, 9, 10) horizontal half blocks leaning from right to left, with 8 (8, 9, 9, 10, 10) sts in each block. Now continue with vertical half blocks at each side and whole blocks alternating direction on each tier. When there are 17 (19, 19, 19, 18, 19) tiers of whole blocks, work 1 tier of horizontal half blocks. **NOTE:** For Size XL, on last tier, work quarter blocks at each side. Place the center 24 (32, 27, 36, 40, 40) sts on a holder for back neck. Set back aside.

Front

With larger circular, using elastic method (see page 16), CO 56 (64, 72, 81, 90, 100) sts. Work back and forth in entrelac as follows: Work 1 tier of 7 (8, 8, 9, 9, 10) horizontal half blocks leaning from right to left, with 8 (8, 9, 9, 10, 10) sts in each block. Now continue with vertical half blocks at each side and whole blocks alternating direction on each tier. When there are 7 (7, 7, 7, 5, 5) tiers of whole blocks, begin working 1 block less at one side on each tier— see schematic.

Place the sts of the blocks leaning from left to right on the right front and from right to left on the left front, on separate holders. These sts will be used later for the bands worked along the V-neck. When there are 17 (19, 19, 19, 18, 19) tiers of whole blocks, set piece aside. Work the opposite front, reversing shaping and decreasing to match first front.

Sleeves

With smaller dpn, using elastic method (see page 16), CO 30 (30, 36, 36, 42, 42) sts. Join to work entrelac in the round; pm for end of rnd. Work 1 tier of 6 horizontal half blocks leaning from right to left, with 5 (5, 6, 6, 7, 7) sts in each block. Work 3 tiers of whole blocks alternating direction on each tier. Next, work 1 tier of horizontal half blocks leaning right to left. Increase evenly spaced around to 40 (40, 48, 48, 56, 56) sts on the first rnd of St st. Change to larger dpn. Continue around in St st until sleeve measures 18½ (18½, 18½, 18½, 18½, 18½) in / 47 (47, 47, 47, 47, 47) cm BUT, at the same time, approx. every ¾ (¾, ¾, ¾, ⅝, ⅝) in / 2 (2, 2, 2, 1.5, 1.5) cm, increase 1 st on each side of the last st of the rnd. When there are 74 (78, 82, 88, 98, 110) sts, BO loosely. Make the second sleeve the same way.

Finishing

Before seaming, *very lightly* steam press the pieces under a damp pressing cloth. Seam the back and fronts at the shoulders. Make sure that the blocks match for best results. Seam the sides, leaving an opening for the tie band on one side. Place the opening 7 (7, 7, 7, 5, 5) whole block tiers up from lower edge. Attach sleeves: sew inside the first stitch loop for a smooth seam.

Tie Bands

Before knitting the bands, we recommend that you try on the garment. Decide how wide you'd like the neck opening. You can adjust it by the width of the band that goes all around the neck and at the lower edge of the front. The band described here, is about 1¼ in / 3 cm wide.

With larger dpn, CO 9 sts. Work back and forth in k1, p1 ribbing for about 41 (42½, 45¼, 48, 50¾, 54) in / 104 (108, 115, 122, 129, 137) cm. Now attach the band to the front as follows: Work all but the last st of the row, place the band next to the diagonal edge of front, pick up a strand in the outermost stitch loop of the front, place new st on needle with band and k2tog. Turn and work row to end. Every time you are at front edge, pick up 1 st through both stitch loops and knit it tog with last st on needle. When you come to sts on a holder, knit each tog with last st of needle instead of picking up a st. Continue the same way along front V-neck, across back neck, and down diagonal edge of opposite front. So that the band won't draw in too much across neck, about every 3rd st, pick up an extra st across front and back neck. Continue as est until the loose end of the band measures 41 (42½, 45¼, 48, 50¾, 54) in / 104 (108, 115, 122, 129, 137) cm. BO loosely and weave in all ends neatly on WS.

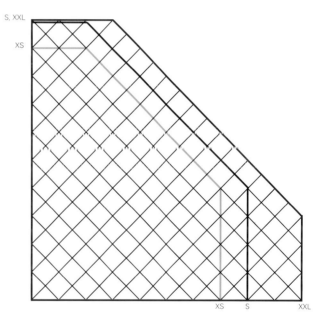

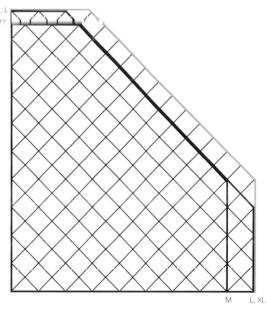

Silja

This easy-to-knit skirt is adaptable for many outfits, occasions, and ages. It's knitted from the top down, which makes it easy to adjust the length. The entrelac makes the skirt very elastic, so it adjusts to any body shape in a pleasing manner. If you want to lengthen the skirt, just work more tiers of whole blocks before you finish with a tier of horizontal half blocks. Don't forget to buy extra yarn if you make the skirt longer.

ADULT SKIRT

SKILL LEVEL: Experienced
SIZES: S (M, L, XL, XXL)
FINISHED MEASUREMENTS
Circumference at Waist: 23¾ (26, 28¼, 33, 35½) in / 60 (66, 72, 84, 90) cm (measured flat without stretching—the skirt is very stretchy)
Total Length: 17¾ (17¾, 18, 20½, 20½) in / 45 (45, 48, 52, 52) cm
MATERIALS
Yarn:
  CYCA #3 (DK, light worsted) Mitu from Rauma (50% wool, 50% alpaca, 109 yd/100 m / 50 g)
Yarn Color and Amounts:
  Ochre 7150 OR Gray Heather SFN43: 200 (250, 250, 300, 300, 350) g
Needles:
  U. S. sizes 2.5 and 6 / 3 and 4 mm: circular
GAUGE
22 sts in St st on larger needles = 4 in / 10 cm. Adjust needle size to obtain correct gauge if necessary.

With smaller circular, CO 120 (132, 144, 156, 168) sts. Join, being careful not to twist cast-on row; pm for beginning of rnd. Work around in k1, p1 ribbing for 3¼ in / 8 cm. Change to larger circular and, on next rnd, knit, decreasing every 4th st evenly spaced around = 90 (99, 108, 117, 126) sts rem. Now begin entrelac in the rnd: Work 1st tier with 10 (11, 12, 13, 14) horizontal half blocks leaning from right to left, with 9 sts in each block.

Tiers 2-3: Work whole blocks with 9 sts in each block.
Tier 4: Increase to 10 sts per whole block.
Tier 5: Work with 10-st whole blocks.
Tier 6: Increase to 11 sts per whole block.
Continue with 11-st whole blocks until you have a total of 9 (9, 10, 11, 11) tiers of whole blocks. Finish with a tier of horizontal half blocks = 110 (121, 132, 143, 154) sts around.

Knit 1 rnd over all sts, increasing evenly spaced around to 120 (132, 144, 156, 168) sts. Work 5 rnds k1, p1 ribbing and then BO in ribbing. Weave in all ends neatly on WS.

Knits for Men

Entrelac is just as nice for men as women. Our two men's sweaters answered our husbands' thoughts on the matter. The only condition was that entrelac had to be included. With a little help, we agreed on these two sweaters with different yarn weights and looks and were very satisfied with the results. The matching hats and mittens were natural accessories.

Loke

SWEATER, HAT, AND MITTENS

Loke is a Norwegian name for a Norse god who makes a lot of mischief. This pullover is knitted in the round in stockinette up to the armholes. The body is then divided for front and back, which are separately worked back and forth in entrelac. An I-cord neckband adds a fine finish to the garment. The sleeves are knitted in stockinette and attached without a facing. Instead of regular ribbing, the cuffs are enhanced with entrelac. What a lovely effect!

The hat (see page 126) is made in one size but can be made bigger by using larger needles. Simple men's mittens (see page 128) with entrelac on the cuffs complement the sweater and hat.

PULLOVER

SKILL LEVEL: Experienced
SIZES: S (M, L, XL, XXL)
FINISHED MEASUREMENTS
Chest: 37¾ (40¼, 42¼, 44½, 47¼) in / 96 (102, 107, 113, 120) cm
Total Length: 27¼ (27½, 28¼, 28¾, 29¼) in / 69 (70, 72, 73, 74) cm
Sleeve Length: 22¾ (22¾, 23¼, 22½, 22) in / 58 (58, 59, 57, 56) cm
MATERIALS
Yarn:
   CYCA #3 (DK, light worsted) Tinde Pelsullgarn from Hillesvåg (100% Norwegian wool, 284 yd/260 m / 100 g)
Yarn Color and Amount:
   Light Denim Blue 652113: 500 (550, 600, 650, 700) g
Needles:
   U. S. sizes 4 and 6 / 3.5 and 4 mm: circulars and, for sleeves, set of 5 dpn
GAUGE
22 sts in St st on smaller needles = 4 in / 10 cm. Adjust needle size to obtain correct gauge if necessary.

Body
With smaller circular and using elastic cast-on method (see page 16), CO 156 (168, 174, 186, 198) sts. Join, being careful not to twist cast-on row; pm for beginning of rnd. Begin working entrelac in the around: Work 26 (28, 29, 31, 33) horizontal half blocks leaning from right to left, with 6 sts in each block. Work 3 tiers of whole blocks, alternating direction of blocks each tier. End with 1 tier of horizontal half blocks. On the next rnd, increase evenly spaced around to 212 (224, 236, 248, 264) sts. Change to larger circular. Work around in St st until body measures 19¼ (19¾, 18½, 19, 19¼) in / 49 (50, 47, 48, 49) cm. On the next rnd, decrease 52 (62, 76, 72, 72) sts evenly spaced around = 160 (162, 160, 176, 192) sts rem. Divide body with 80 (81, 80, 88, 96) sts each for front and back. Work front and back separately.

Back
Working back and forth, work 1 tier with 8 (9, 8, 8, 8) horizontal half blocks leaning from right to left, with 8 (9, 10, 11, 12) sts in each block. Now work vertical half blocks at each side, first picking up 1 st between the first block of front and last block of back at each side for edge sts of the vertical half blocks.

Continue with 8 (8, 7, 6, 6) tiers of whole blocks alternating direction of blocks each tier. End with 1 tier of horizontal half blocks. Place sts of the 4 (4, 4, 3, 3) horizontal half blocks (= total of 32 (36, 40, 33, 36) sts) on a holder for back neck.

Shoulders: BO loosely, but, *at the same time*, M1 after every 3rd st; BO new sts in sequence. This technique produces an elastic edge.

Front
Work as for back to a total of 6 (6, 5, 4, 4) tiers of whole blocks. On the next row, work as shown on the schematic below.

Tier 7 (7, 6, 5, 5):
Sizes S and M: Work 1 vertical half block, 3 whole blocks, 2 horizontal half blocks, 3 whole blocks, and 1 vertical half block. Place sts from the horizontal half blocks on a holder.
Size L: Work 3 whole blocks, 2 horizontal half blocks, 3 whole blocks. Place sts from the horizontal half blocks on a holder.
Sizes XL and XXL: Work 1 vertical half block, 3 whole blocks, 1 horizontal half block, 3 whole blocks, and 1 vertical half block. Place sts from the horizontal half blocks on a holder.

Work each shoulder separately.

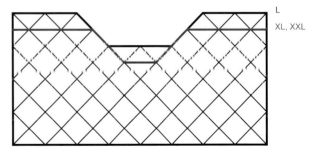

L
XL, XXL

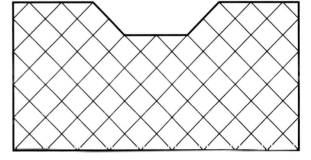

S, M

Left Shoulder
Work from left to right.

Tier 8 (8, 7, 6, 6):
Sizes S and M: Work 3 whole blocks.
Size L: Work 1 vertical half block and 2 whole blocks.
Sizes XL and XXL: Work 3 whole blocks.

Tier 9 (9, 8, 7, 7):
Sizes S and M: Work 1 quarter block and 2 horizontal half blocks.
Size L: Work 2 horizontal half blocks.
Sizes XL and XXL: Work 1 quarter block and 2 horizontal half blocks.

BO loosely as for back.

Right Shoulder
Work as for left shoulder, reversing shaping to correspond.

Sleeves
With smaller dpn and using elastic cast-on method (see page 16), CO 36 (36, 42, 42, 48) sts. Divide sts onto dpn and join; pm for beginning of rnd. Begin with entrelac in the round: Work 6 (6, 7, 7, 8) horizontal half blocks leaning from right to left, with 6 sts in each block.

Work 3 tiers of whole blocks, alternating direction of blocks each tier. End with 1 tier horizontal half blocks.

Knit 1 rnd, increasing evenly spaced around to 50 (52, 54, 56, 58) sts. Change to larger dpn and St st. Approx. every ¾ in / 2 cm, increase 1 st on each side of 1st st of rnd to a total of 90 (96, 100, 106, 112) sts. Continue until sleeve measures 22¾ (22¾, 23¼, 22½, 22) in / 58 (58, 59, 57, 56) cm. BO loosely. Make the second sleeve the same way.

Finishing
Seam shoulders, working inside first stitch loop.

Neckband: Place sts of back neck onto smaller circular, pick up and knit sts through both stitch loops at each side of neck, and place sts of center front onto needle for a total of 80 (90, 100, 110, 120) sts. Work I-cord bind-off (see page 16).

We recommend that, before attaching sleeves, you steam press the entrelac on the sleeves *very lightly*

as the cuffs are drawn in now but will flatten out as the sweater is worn. Attach sleeves. The armholes may be larger than the sleeve tops. Pin the center of the sleeve at the shoulder seam and sew down from that point on each side, and close any remaining opening at underarm. Weave in all ends neatly on WS.

HAT

SKILL LEVEL: Experienced
SIZE: Men's (sizing adjustable by changing gauge)
MATERIALS
Yarn:
  CYCA #3 (DK, light worsted) Tinde Pelsullgarn from Hillesvåg (100% Norwegian wool, 284 yd/260 m / 100 g)
Yarn Color and Amount:
  Light Denim Blue 652113: 100 g
Needles:
  U. S. size 4 / 3.5 mm: short circular or set of 5 dpn
GAUGE
22 sts in St st = 4 in / 10 cm.
Adjust needle size to obtain correct gauge if necessary.

CO 108 sts. Join, being careful not to twist cast-on row; pm for beginning of rnd. Work around in k2, p2 ribbing for 1½ in / 4 cm. Knit 1 rnd, decreasing evenly spaced around to 88 sts. Now begin entrelac in the round. Work 1 tier of 11 horizontal half blocks leaning from right to left, with 8 sts in each block. Continue with 5 tiers of whole blocks, alternating direction of blocks each tier. Finish with a "star" shaping (see page 15). Weave in all ends neatly on WS.

MITTENS

SKILL LEVEL: Experienced
SIZE: Men's
MATERIALS
Yarn:
  CYCA #3 (DK, light worsted) Tinde Pelsullgarn from Hillesvåg (100% Norwegian wool, 284 yd/260 m / 100 g)
Yarn Color and Amount:
  Light Denim Blue 652113: 100 g
Needles:
  U. S. size 4 / 3.5 mm: set of 5 dpn
GAUGE
22 sts in St st = 4 in / 10 cm.
Adjust needle size to obtain correct gauge if necessary.

_____

Both Mittens

CO 48 sts and divide evenly onto 4 dpn. Join and knit 8 rnds. Next, knit 1 rnd, decreasing every 4th st to 36 sts [= (K2, k2tog) around]. Now work entrelac in the round: Work 6 horizontal half blocks leaning from right to left, with 6 sts in each block. Continue with 3 tiers of whole blocks, alternating direction of blocks each tier. End entrelac with 1 tier of horizontal half blocks. Knit 1 rnd, increasing evenly spaced around to 48 sts. Work 6 rnds k1, p1 ribbing.

Left-Hand Mitten

Continue around in St st. On the 2nd rnd after the ribbing, begin shaping the thumb gusset as follows:

Increase Rnd 1: Increase 1 st on each side of the next-to-last st of rnd. Increase with yo which will be worked through back loop on next rnd.
Knit 2 rnds.
Increase Rnd 2: Yo before and after the previous new sts = yo, k3, yo.
Knit 2 rnds.
Increase Rnd 3: Yo before and after the previous new sts = yo, k5, yo.
Knit 2 rnds.
Work a total of 5 increase rnds with 2 knit rnds in between = 11 thumb gusset sts.
Knit 3 rnds without increasing. Place thumb gusset sts on a holder + 1 st at each side = 13 sts on holder. CO 3 new sts over gap and then continue in St st for 3½ in / 9 cm or to desired length to tip of little finger.

Top Shaping: Divide the sts evenly onto 4 dpn (= 12 sts on each needle), beginning rnd at start of Ndl 1 (= tip of little finger). Decrease as follows on every rnd:
Ndls 1 and 3: K9, k2tog, k1.
Ndls 2 and 4: K1, sl 1, k1, psso or ssk, k9.
There will be 1 st less on each needle on every rnd. When 8 sts total rem, cut yarn. Draw end through rem sts and tighten.

Thumb

Slip held thumb sts to dpn and pick up and knit 5 sts along top of thumbhole = 18 sts.
Work around in St st for about 2½ in / 6.5 cm. Work k2tog around and around until 8 sts rem. Cut yarn and draw end through rem sts; tighten.

Right-Hand Mitten

Work as for left mitten, reversing placement of thumb gusset: begin increases on each side of 2nd st of rnd.

Balder

PULLOVER WITH COLLAR AND HAT
Balder is the name of the Norse god of
light, a son of Odin. This pullover features a
wide entrelac panel on both front and back
with the rest of the body in stockinette. The
front and back are each worked separately,
back and forth. The sleeves are also
worked back and forth and have a stripe
of entrelac blocks up the middle of each
sleeve. The sleeves are sewn in afterwards.
The Balder hat (see page 134) is a fine
accessory to wear with the sweater.

PULLOVER

SKILL LEVEL: Experienced
SIZES: XS (S, M, L, XL, XXL)
FINISHED MEASUREMENTS
Chest: 36¾ (39, 42¼, 46, 50, 51½) in / 93 (99, 107, 117,
   127, 131) cm
Total Length: 24½ (25¼, 26, 27½, 28¼, 29¼) in / 62
   (64, 66, 70, 72, 74) cm
Sleeve Length: 19¼ (19¾, 20, 20, 20½, 21) in / 49 (50,
   51, 51, 52, 53) cm
MATERIALS
Yarn:
   CYCA #5 (bulky) Blåne Pelsullgarn from Hifa (100%
   wool, 125 yd/114 m / 100 g) OR Vams PT3 from
   Rauma (100% wool, 90 yd/82 m / 50 g)
Yarn Color and Amount:
   Blåne Pelsull Natural Gray 672115: 850 (900, 950,
   1000, 1050, 1100) g
   OR Vams PT3 White V00: 600 (650, 700, 750, 800,
   850) g
Needles:
   U. S. sizes 8 and 10 / 5 and 6 mm: circulars and sets
   of 5 dpn
GAUGE
14 sts in St st on larger needles = 4 in / 10 cm.
Adjust needle size to obtain correct gauge if
necessary.

Back
With smaller circular, CO 68 (72, 78, 84, 90, 94) sts.
Work back and forth in k1, p1 ribbing for 1½ in / 4
cm. Change to larger needle. Purl 1 row *at the same*

time decreasing (evenly spaced across) the center 40 (40, 40, 46, 46, 46) sts to 30 (30, 30, 35, 35, 35) sts = 58 (62, 68, 73, 79, 83) sts rem. The center 30 (30, 30, 35, 35, 35) sts will now be worked in entrelac. On each side of the entrelac panel, work k1, p5, and 8 (10, 13, 13, 16, 18) sts of St st, *at the same time* as working vertical half blocks (see schematics on page 132).

Begin the entrelac with 6 (6, 6, 7, 7, 7) horizontal half blocks leaning from right to left, with 5 sts in each block. Continue with tiers of whole blocks with a vertical half block at each side.

When piece measures 24½ (25¼, 26, 27½, 28¼, 29¼) in / 62 (64, 66, 70, 72, 74) cm or has 1 tier of horizontal half blocks + 23 (24, 25, 26, 27, 28) tiers of whole blocks, end piece with 1 tier of horizontal half blocks over the entrelac panel. Set piece aside.

Front
Work as for back until piece measures 15½ (16¼, 17, 17¾, 18½, 19) in / 39 (41, 43, 45, 47, 48) cm or has 1 tier horizontal half blocks + 14 (15, 16, 17, 18, 19) tiers of whole blocks. Now work horizontal half blocks over the center 4 (4, 4, 5, 5, 5) blocks. Loosely BO the center 4 (4, 4, 5, 5, 5) entrelac blocks. Continue on shoulders until front is same total length as back.

Sleeves
The sleeves are worked back and forth in St st with a stripe of entrelac over the center sts. With smaller needle (or dpn), CO 34 (36, 38, 38, 40, 40) sts. Work in k1, p1 ribbing for 1½ (2, 1½, 2, 1½, 2) in / 4 (5, 4, 5, 4, 5) cm.

Change to larger needle. Work 1 row in St st, *at the same time* decreasing 1 st over the center 6 sts – 5 sts at center for the entrelac panel. Work 1 horizontal half block with 5 sts in the block. On the next tier, work 2 vertical half blocks. On each side of the entrelac panel, work k1, p5 with the rest of the row in St st (see schematic on page 132). The st at each side of the entrelac panel is knitted together with the vertical half block.

Continue working the tiers, alternating 1 whole block and 2 vertical half blocks. *At the same time*, increase 1 st at each side of the last st of the row every 1¼ in / 3 cm until there are 23 (24, 25, 26, 27, 28) sts of St st on each side of entrelac panel. Continue as est until sleeve measures 19¼ (19¾, 20, 20, 20½, 21) in / 49 (50, 51, 51, 52, 53) cm or has 1 horizontal half block + 8 (8, 9, 9, 10, 10) whole blocks. End with one horizontal half block and then BO loosely. Make the second sleeve the same way.

Finishing
Before knitting collar, seam the shoulders. The sts held from back neck will be used for the collar.
Collar: With smaller needle, pick up and knit 35 (35, 35, 37, 37, 37) sts along each side of the neck, as well as the 20 (20, 20, 25, 25, 25) sts of back neck. Work back and forth in k1, p1 ribbing over these 90 (90, 90, 99, 99, 99) sts. When collar measures 2 in / 5 cm, increase over the 26 sts at center back as follows: Work 26 (26, 26, 23, 23, 23) sts, increase 2 sts in the next st and then in every 3rd st another 12 times; complete row. Make the increases with yo on each side of the "increase" st. Work increases into ribbing on next row (some sts may be changed to knit or purl in sequence). Continue in ribbing until collar is as wide as front neck. The collar overlaps completely from side to side (see photo opposite).

Attach sleeves; seam underarms and sides. Weave in all ends neatly on WS.

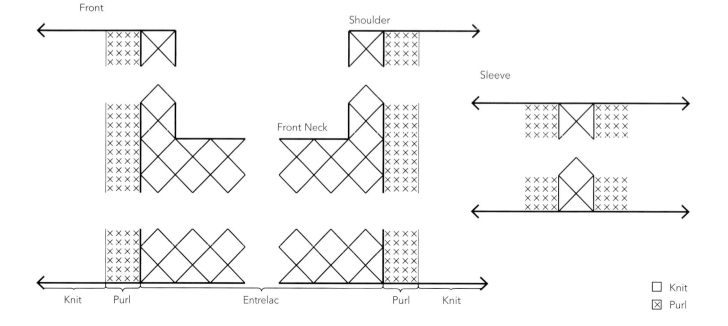

Front

Shoulder

Sleeve

Front Neck

Knit   Purl   Entrelac   Purl   Knit

☐ Knit
☒ Purl

HAT

This hat is an excellent accessory to wear with the Balder Pullover. You can adjust the sizing by changing the gauge. (If you want a smaller hat, work with U. S. size 8 / 5 mm needles; for a larger one, try U. S. size 9 or 10 / 5.5 or 6 mm.)

SKILL LEVEL: Experienced
SIZE: Men's
MATERIALS
Yarn:
 CYCA #5 (Bulky) Blåne Pelsullgarn from Hifa (100% wool, 125 yd/114 m / 100 g) OR Vams PT3 from Rauma (100% wool, 90 yd/82 m / 50 g)
Yarn Color and Amount:
 Blåne Pelsull Natural Gray 672115: 100 g
 OR Vams PT3 White V00: 100 g
Needles:
 U. S. size 8 / 5 mm: set of 5 dpn
GAUGE
14 sts in St st = 4 in / 10 cm.
Adjust needle size to obtain correct gauge if necessary.

CO 72 sts. Divide sts onto 4 dpn and join; pm for beginning of rnd. Work in k2, p2 ribbing for 1½ in / 4 cm. Next, knit 1 rnd, decreasing evenly spaced around to 50 sts. Work around in entrelac: Work 1 tier of 10 horizontal half blocks leaning from right to left with 5 sts in each block. Work 6 tiers of whole blocks. Finish with a "star" shaping (see page 15). Weave in all ends neatly on WS.

Furnishings

Entrelac can also be used for interior decoration. It's never a mistake to have some pretty pillows and a lovely throw on the sofa. Entrelac provides a graphic element to enhance the elegant effect.

Edda

PILLOW COVERS

"Edda" is the name for two 13th-century collections of Norse mythology and epic poetry. Round pillow covers are rather easy to knit. One pillow is rarely enough, so why not knit several in a variety of colors and sizes to match your interior? We made two pillows, one square and one oblong. They can be paired or used singly.

SQUARE PILLOW COVER

SKILL LEVEL: Experienced
FINISHED MEASUREMENTS
19¾ x 19¾ in / 50 x 50 cm
MATERIALS
Yarn:
   CYCA #6 (super bulky) Drops Andes from
   Garnstudio (65% wool, 35% alpaca, 105 yd/96 m /
   100 g)
Yarn Color and Amount:
   Orange 2920: 500 g
Other Materials:
   Insert pillow same size as or slightly larger than
   pillow cover
Needles:
   U. S. size 11 / 8 mm: circular
GAUGE
10 sts in St st = 4 in / 10 cm.
Adjust needle size to obtain correct gauge if
necessary.

With elastic method (see page 16), CO 77 sts.
Join, being careful not to twist cast-on row; pm for
beginning of rnd. Work around in entrelac: Work 1
tier of 11 horizontal half blocks leaning from right
to left, with 7 sts in each block. Now work 10 tiers
of whole blocks, alternating direction of blocks on
each tier. End with 1 tier of horizontal half blocks. BO
loosely, but, *at the same time*, M1 after every 3rd st;
BO new sts in sequence. This technique produces an
elastic edge.

Finishing
Seam the top of the cover inside the bind-off row,
making sure that the blocks match. For seaming
the lower edge, you have several choices. We
recommend sewing the edge on each side slightly
inside the edge and then crocheting a looped edge
of chain sts along both sides. Finally, we make a
twisted yarn cord. We thread the cord through the
loops on the bias, tighten, tie the yarn and insert the
inner pillow. This way, you have an almost invisible
closure that won't be a problem when the pillow
needs to be washed, and you avoid adding a stiff
zipper which will only be in the way.

OBLONG PILLOW COVER

SKILL LEVEL: Experienced
FINISHED MEASUREMENTS
15¾ x 23¾ in / 40 x 60 cm
MATERIALS
Yarn:
   CYCA #6 (super bulky) Drops Andes from
   Garnstudio (65% wool, 35% alpaca, 105 yd/96 m /
   100 g)
Yarn Color and Amount:
   White 1101: 300 g
   Black 8903: 300 g
Other Materials:
   Insert pillow same size as or slightly larger than
   pillow cover
Needles:
   U. S. size 11 / 8 mm: circular
GAUGE
10 sts in St st = 4 in / 10 cm.
Adjust needle size to obtain correct gauge if
necessary.

With White and elastic method (see page 16), CO 112
sts. Join, being careful not to twist cast-on row; pm
for beginning of rnd. Work around in entrelac: Work
1 tier of 16 horizontal half blocks leaning from right to
left, with 7 sts in each block. Change to Black. Now
work in whole blocks alternating colors and direction
of blocks on each tier. Work a total of 9 tiers of whole
blocks; the last tier should be Black. End with 1 tier
of horizontal half blocks with White. BO loosely, but,
at the same time, M1 after every 3rd st; BO new sts in
sequence. This technique produces an elastic edge.

Finishing
Seam and insert pillow as for square cover.

- 139 -

Hegelin's Throw

This throw originated with a woman who was taking a class on entrelac at the Norddal Handicraft Association in 2014. It's a large project, but simple, and still suitable for a beginner. It consists of 20 squares joined into a large blanket. The six variations of the pattern squares combine for a delightful effect.

SKILL LEVEL: Experienced
FINISHED MEASUREMENTS
55 x 69 in / 140 x 175 cm. Each square measures 13¾ x 13¾ in / 35 x 35 cm.
MATERIALS
Yarn:
   CYCA #5 (bulky) Puno from Rauma (68% alpaca, 22% nylon, 10% Merino wool, 120 yd/110 m / 50 g)
Yarn Color and Amount:
   Light Gray 1310: 1300 g
Needles:
   U. S. size 11 / 8 mm: circular
GAUGE
10 sts in St st = 4 in / 10 cm.
Adjust needle size to obtain correct gauge if necessary.

This throw consists of 20 squares, 4 across and 5 in length. Divide up the patterns as you like.
NOTE: Squares 1 and 6 are difficult to knit to the correct size. You may need to go up a needle size for Square 1 and down a size for Square 6. Alternatively, you can make the blanket with Squares 2-5 only.

All the squares: Using the elastic method (see page 16), CO 32 sts for an edge st on each side and 30 sts for the entrelac patterning. The edge sts are worked

together with the vertical half blocks. Work the entrelac as described for each square. Loosely BO purlwise on WS.

Square 1: Work 1 tier of 10 horizontal half blocks with 3 sts in each block. Work 19 tiers of whole blocks and end with 1 tier of horizontal half blocks.
Square 2: Work 1 tier of 6 horizontal half blocks with 5 sts in each block. Work 11 tiers of whole blocks and end with 1 tier of horizontal half blocks.
Square 3: Work 1 tier of 5 horizontal half blocks with 6 sts in each block. Work 9 tiers of whole blocks and end with 1 tier of horizontal half blocks.
Square 4: Work 1 tier of 3 horizontal half blocks with 10 sts in each block. Work 5 tiers of whole blocks and end with 1 tier of horizontal half blocks.
Square 5: Work 1 tier of 2 horizontal half blocks with 15 sts in each block. Work 3 tiers of whole blocks and end with 1 tier of horizontal half blocks.
Square 6: Work 1 tier of 1 horizontal half block with 30 sts in each block. Work 1 tier with 2 vertical half blocks and end with 1 tier of 1 horizontal half block.

Finishing
Neatly sew all the squares together. Weave in all ends neatly on WS.

ACKNOWLEDGMENTS

Thank You

To our fantastic test-knitters:
Kari Kvilvang, Anne Gry Sandmark Moen, Gerd Jorun Igland, Thea Camilla Hansen Fürst, Heidi Storstad, Ruth-Tove Sletten, Therese Kristoffersen, Kristin Stensland, Margrethe Ulvatne, Aud Brynjulfsen and Maria Danielsen Myhre.

To Rauma Yarn, Hillesvåg Ullvarefabrikk, and Two Knitting Women for wonderful yarn and quick service. To Hegelin Waldal for the inspiration for Hegelin's Throw.

To the photo models who so willingly lined up and smiled prettily no matter how cold it was:
Britt Ekrum Melchior, Nina Sjøblom, Anne-Marie Sjøblom, Adrian Krogsæter, Karsten Eikeland, Mikkel and Oskar, Angelika and Annika, Hege Hovden, Synne Hovden, Tuva Eikeland, and Oda Eikeland.

To Härstua (a hair salon), who took us in to warm up and let the models change during the long photo sessions; and to Kafè Under Taket, for spontaneously letting us take photos of the Mist sweater in the café.

To Livø Moen Eikeland for the wonderful job with the photography and Laila Sundet Gundersen for graphic design. To Kaja Marie Lereng Kvernbakken who was a very useful fact checker and proofreader, to Cappelen Damm who believed in us, and editor Toril Blomquist who brought our ship safely into port. Thanks also to our good designer friends who have cheered us on.

To our families, who wondered if we would ever have occasional conversations with them again—and if we might sometimes talk about something other than entrelac, yarn, needles, and everything else having to do with this knitting book.

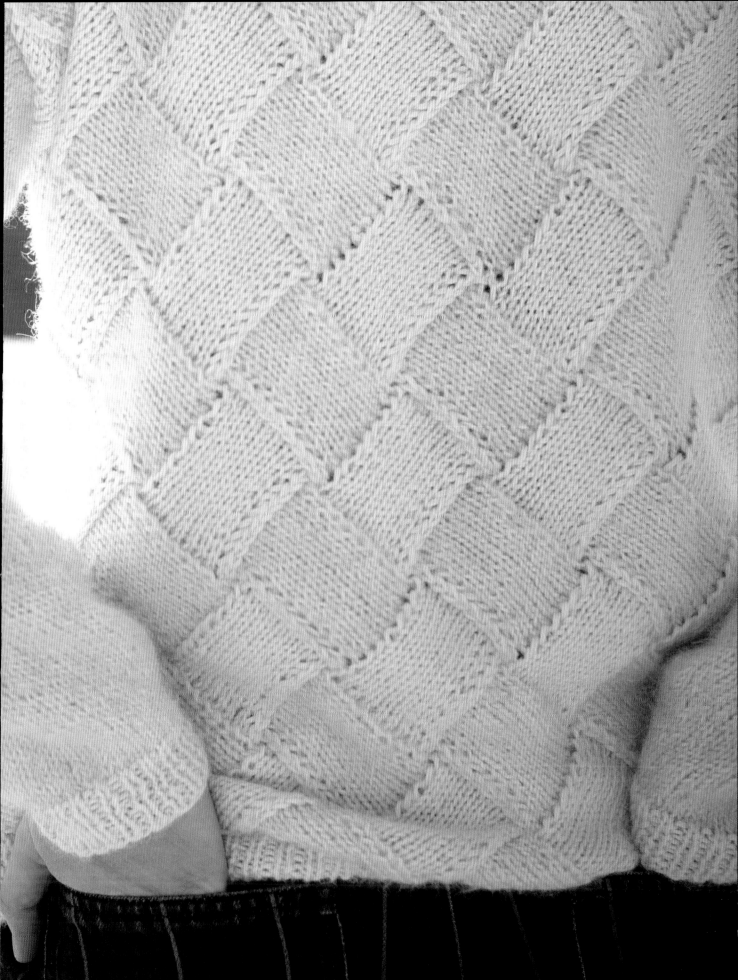

RESOURCES

• Amoriza, Silje Een De og Myrstad, Ingrid:
*Vintagestrikk. Strikkeoppskrifter for smarte klær til alle
og enhver 1935–1955* [Vintage Knitting. Knitting Patterns
for Chic Clothes for Everyone]. Spartacus 2013.
• Bolstad, Ruth Gullbekk: *Kontstrikk* [Entrelac Knitting].
Unika Forlag 2008.
• Eikeland, Heidi and Hovden, Mette: *Kontstrikk,
enklere enn du tror* [Entrelac: Easier than You Think].
Licentia 2015.
• Grasmane, Maruta: *Mittens of Latvia*. National
Costume Center Sena Klets 2015.
• Saglie, Gjertrud: *Strikke—hekle—binde* [Knit—
Crochet—Nålbind]. Landbruksforlaget 1989.
• Vottelauget: *Eventyrvotter* [Fantasy Mittens].
Aschehoug 2015.

SOURCES OF INSPIRATION
• Bortner, Gwen: *Entrée to Entrelac*. XRX 2010.
• Drysdale, Rosemary: *Entrelac: The Essential Guide to
Interlace Knitting*. Sixth&Spring 2010.
• Drysdale, Rosemary: *Entrelac 2: New Techniques for
Interlace Knitting*. Sixth&Spring 2014.

Podcasts we recommend for listening to while you knit:
• KnitBritish (knitbritish.net).
• The Yarniacs (yarniacs.blogspot.com).
• Fruity Knitting (fruityknitting.com).

———————————

If you need advice or help with entrelac knitting,
check our Facebook group: "Kontstrikk, enklere enn
du tror," or contact us at pinnedans@gmail.com. You
can also find us at pinnedans.com, our Facebook page:
Pinnedans, and our Instagram account @pinnedans.

YARN INFORMATION

• Garnstudio yarns may be purchased from retailers
listed by: **Garnstudio** (garnstudio.com)
• Hillesvåg yarns may be purchased (with international
shipping charges) from: **Ysolda** (ysolda.com)
• Rauma yarns are available from: **The Yarn Guys**
(theyarnguys.com)
• Sandnes yarns may be purchased (with international
shipping charges) from: **Scandinavian Knitting Design**
(scandinavianknittingdesign.com)

Some yarns—Hifa yarns and Viking yarns, in
particular—may be difficult to find. A variety of
additional and substitute yarns are available from:
• **Deramores** (deramores.com)
• **LoveCrafts** (lovecrafts.com)
• **Wool Warehouse** (woolwarehouse.co.uk)

———————————

If you are unable to obtain any of the yarn used in this
book, it can be replaced with a yarn of similar weight
and composition. Please note, however, that the
finished products may vary slightly from those shown,
depending on the yarn used. Try yarnsub.com for
suggestions.

For more information on selecting or substituting yarn,
contact your local yarn shop or an online store; they are
familiar with all types of yarns and would be happy to
help you. Additionally, the online knitting community at
Ravelry.com has forums where you can post questions
about specific yarns. Yarns come and go so quickly these
days, and there are so many beautiful yarns available.